Lia Slofstra

D0825447

The Little Coat

The Bob and Sue Elliott Story

Alan J. Buick

1212

ELIZABETH K SLOFSTRA
4382 54A AVE CLOSE
INNISFAIL AB
T4G 1X5

The Little Coat

The Bob and Sue Elliott Story

Alan J. Buick

DriverWorks Ink
www.driverworks.ca

© Alan J. Buick, 2009

All rights reserved. No part of this work may be reproduced or transmitted in any form or by any means – graphic, electronic or mechanic, including photocopying, recording, taping or information storage and retrieval systems – without the prior written permission of the publisher or a licence from the Canadian Copyright Licensing Agency (Access Copyright).

Library and Archives Canada Cataloguing in Publication

Buick, Alan J., 1945-
The little coat : the Bob and Sue Elliott story / Alan J. Buick.

Includes bibliographical references.
ISBN 978-0-9810394-3-5

1. Elliott, Bob, 1925-. 2. Elliott, Sue, 1934-. 3. World War, 1939- 1945--Netherlands. 4. Netherlands--History--German occupation, 1940-1945. 5. Cretier family. 6. Canada. Canadian Army--Biography. 7. Soldiers--Canada--Biography. 8. World War, 1939-1945--Personal narratives, Canadian. I. Title.

D811.E45 2009   940.54'8171   C2009-906229-1

Editor and book design – Deana Driver
Front cover photo – Child's wool coat, CWM 20060093-001,
© Canadian War Museum
Back cover photo – Tulips – Jack Malagride
Back cover photos – Bob and Sue Elliott
Author photo – Jason Grover
All other photos courtesy of Bob and Sue Elliott except as noted.

The publisher gratefully acknowledges the financial assistance of the Saskatchewan Publishers Group through the Creative Enterprise Entrepreneurship Fund and all those who pre-ordered a book.
Printed and bound in Canada.

ENVIRONMENTAL BENEFITS STATEMENT

DriverWorks Ink saved the following resources by printing the pages of this book on chlorine free paper made with 100% post-consumer waste.

TREES	WATER	SOLID WASTE	GREENHOUSE GASES
40 FULLY GROWN	18,411 GALLONS	1,118 POUNDS	3,823 POUNDS

Calculations based on research by Environmental Defense and the Paper Task Force.
Manufactured at Friesens Corporation

Mixed Sources
Cert no. SW-COC-001271
© 1996 FSC
FSC

DriverWorks Ink
Saskatchewan, Canada   www.driverworks.ca   (306) 545-5293

www.thelittlecoat.com

Contents

PROLOGUE

August 1944

"What is this garbage?!" the German officer barked at Willem Cretier, his face contorted with rage. "Don't you know that Prince Bernhard is nothing but a bum? And this is the bum's mother-in-law!"

Willem's wife Geert and their three children had been watching this scene in a state of terror. They did not move.

"Where did you get this thing?" the soldier yelled as he waved the offending poster at Willem. "You will tell me or I will shoot you right now!"

Willem remained silent but his mind was racing. 'Is this the end?' he thought. 'Am I about to die for placing a picture of my beloved queen on the wall in my own home? I have done a lot of things to thwart the Nazis, but this is crazy. I should have listened to Geert and Sussie. They said it would be risky pinning that picture in our living room. I didn't think the damn Germans would see it!'

The officer drew his pistol and ordered Willem outside.

"Form a firing squad!" he shouted to his men. He shoved Willem up against the wall of his own workshop and proceeded to arrange the execution.

Ten-year-old Sussie felt like she was having a nightmare. The kind where you try to run from something terrible but your legs won't work and you feel frozen to the spot. This couldn't be happening. But it was.

Sussie saw the fear in her father's eyes and frantically started to scream at the Germans. "You can't shoot my father! You just can't. He didn't do anything wrong! He didn't put that poster on the wall! I did! I found the flyer! I found it by the dyke!"

She was sobbing uncontrollably now. She fell to her knees and begged the officer, "Please don't kill my father! What would we do without him? If you have to kill someone, kill me! I'm the one who did this."

The officer stared down at Sussie for what seemed like an eternity. Then something softened in his eyes as he watched this act of bravery from such a tiny girl.

"Lower your rifles," he ordered, his tone of voice mellowing as he spoke. "There'll be no execution here today... But you!" he roared at Willem. "Don't you forget this! And make sure your children obey the law! We will be watching you!"

With that, the officer ordered the platoon to fall in and then he barked for them to march away.

Sussie didn't wait to see what happened next. She just ran as hard as she could to her special spot on the dyke by the Waal River. It had been her favourite place to watch the ships go by. She had always felt at peace with the world there – before the Germans came.

Sussie didn't know how long she sat in that spot crying. She just cried and cried, until there were no tears left.

CHAPTER ONE

Fall 1939 –
Before the Germans came

In 1939, Rossum was a small town by Dutch standards with a population of about 1,200 people. Located about an hour south of Amsterdam in the province of Gelderland, it was bordered by the Waal River to its north and the Maas River to its south. These two slow-moving rivers wound their way across the Netherlands[1], providing shipping routes to the inland cities. On the east side of Rossum, the rivers met through a one-kilometre canal with locks that provided ships and barges access from one river's level to the other. The dyke along this canal was one of Sussie's favourite spots to play and relax.

The town of Rossum was typical of those in the region with its beautiful gardens and well-kept houses. Neighbours were friends or relatives and everyone helped each other when needed. Willem and Gerdina (Geert) Cretier were a typical small-town Dutch couple. They grew up in Rossum and were married there in 1931. They lived in a small brick house near the centre of town, about a five-minute walk from the dyke on the Waal River. Their lives were simple and their family was the most important element of each day. Their son Kees was born in 1932. Their daughter Everdina was born two years later in May 1934 and son Gerard was born in 1935.

When Everdina was a baby, Kees loved to push her pram when the family went for walks. If people asked his sister's

---

[1]Holland is a region in the western part of the Netherlands. The name 'Holland' is also often used to refer to the whole of the Netherlands, but this is not formally correct. (www.wikipedia.org)

name, Kees could not say 'Everdina,' so he just said, "Zusje, I have a Zusje," the Dutch word for 'sister.' This name evolved into Sussie and later became Sue. Sussie was a bright, energetic child whose fighting spirit and enthusiasm for life would stay with her through the years.

Willem was the provider for the Cretier family and was well known in the region for his mechanical expertise. People came from far away to ask him to service their vehicles. His brick workshop was small but it was well built in a common style from that period, with two layers of brick separated by a cavity of air that served as insulation. The shop had a tile roof and was close to their home, which was built in the same style. Willem enjoyed the convenience of working so close to his house, walking only a few metres to get to work. He was a tidy man and had a superbly organized workshop.

Willem also owned a half share in a small local bus company. Willem serviced the buses and his partner, a bus driver, was responsible for their operation. The incomes from these two jobs provided well for Willem and his family.

Willem Cretier was a gentle man who could be stern with his children when necessary. Sussie and her brothers were not allowed inside Willem's shop unless they agreed to sit very still and watch their father at work. Willem did not want them to get in his way or worse, to get injured. Sitting still was often difficult for five-year-old Sussie. She had always been inquisitive, adventurous and busy. But she respected her father and listened to his instructions.

As a wife, mother and homemaker, Geert Cretier always put her family's needs first. She had an infectious smile and a magical way of making her children feel important. Sussie loved her mother with all her heart and soul. To Sussie's mind, there was no better mom in the whole world, and certainly no one who could cook better.

Sussie's grandfather on her mother's side managed a brick kiln in the town of Hurwenen, just west of Rossum. Visiting

Opa and watching the bricks being made was a fascinating pastime for young Sussie. Her grandmother had a teahouse there by the river. Sussie loved to sit and watch the ships go by while drinking tea with Oma on warm summer evenings. Sussie loved spending time with her grandparents. She was sure that she not only had a super family but lived in a wonderful country full of history and surprises.

Rope skipping was also a favourite pastime for Sussie and her siblings. They would often skip through town with a crowd of their friends, entertaining themselves with stories and games along the way. Their family pet, a huge Newfoundland dog named Tommy, was their constant companion wherever they went. Whenever Sussie felt sad or discouraged, the friendly dog was there to comfort her. Most of Sussie's spare time was spent with her brothers, though, and they usually found many ways to entertain themselves.

One beautiful fall evening, the Cretier children were playing in their back yard. The flowers of summer were mostly gone along with the fragrance they provided, but the fruits on the apple and plum trees were ripening perfectly. Sussie reached up into the plum tree and picked the best fruit she could see and then sat down on the grass next to Tommy. She leaned back on the dog, got comfortable and took a juicy bite. "These plums are sooo good," she said.

Four-year-old Gerard wasn't paying attention to Sussie. He was looking at the apple trees next door in the neighbour's yard. "Those apples look better than ours," he said aloud.

Sussie quickly reminded her brother that going into the yard next door was not a good idea. "If you get caught over there, you'll be in big trouble with the neighbour. And Dad will be mad at you, too."

Just then, their mother called them in for supper. Sussie and Kees quickly went into the house, but Gerard did not follow.

"Where is Gerard?" Geert asked as they all sat down at the table.

"He was with us in the yard just a minute ago," Kees responded.

The family waited a few minutes, but Gerard did not appear.

"We had better go and look for him," Geert said with a touch of anxiety in her voice.

They looked in the back yard but found no sign of him.

"Gerard, Gerard!" they called. No answer.

Just then, the neighbour whose apples Gerard had admired from afar came around the corner of the Cretiers' house with the missing child in tow. "Look what I found tangled up in the fence," he said to Geert. "He couldn't go forward or back. It's a good thing I found him or he might have been there all night."

Gerard ran to his mother and received a large hug. "Thank goodness you're all right," Geert said with a sigh of relief. "How did you get stuck in there?"

Gerard didn't answer and gave Sussie a quick 'don't-say-anything' look so she wouldn't tell on him either. Sussie looked at her younger brother and decided to keep quiet. He was obviously scared, with big tears in his eyes and a quivering lip. He was lucky that his mom and dad did not pursue an answer to the question but just took their scared little boy into the house where they all ate their supper.

One other day, when Sussie was young, the children found some old wooden shoes and decided to make boats out of them. They painted the shoes and made sails out of old sheets, and even gave their boats names. Then they sailed these makeshift wooden boats in the creek and had races to see whose boat was the fastest.

Kees, Sussie and Gerard had to run fast to keep up with the little boats. During one race, Sussie slipped and fell into the creek. The banks were steep and slippery and although Sussie tried frantically to grab the grass on the sides of the banks, the current was too strong and she pulled handfuls of grass out by the roots as the water dragged her along.

"Help!" she yelled. "Please help me!"

Kees looked around desperately for someone to help Sussie but there was nobody else there except little Gerard. Kees realized he would have to do something or Sussie would drown, and he couldn't let that happen. Running along the edge of the creek, his heart pounding with anxiety, Kees finally found a long piece of wood and held it out to Sussie.

"Grab hold of this!" he yelled at her.

Sussie managed to grasp the wood and hold on tight while Kees guided her to a place where she could get out.

"Mom's going to be really mad at me," Sussie said as she assessed her condition. Her clothes were a mess and she was soaking wet. She was more concerned about displeasing her mother than she was about her brush with death.

"Why don't we go to the neighbour's place and dry you off before we go home?" Kees suggested. So they did.

A while later, Sussie was sitting on the grass letting the sun dry her off when her mother came around the side of the garage. "What are you doing there?" Geert asked, noticing Sussie's wet condition.

'Oh no,' Sussie thought. 'I had better tell the truth because Mom will find out anyway.'

"I fell into the creek when we were racing our boats," Sussie answered, thinking, 'I'm in big trouble now.'

But instead of yelling at her, Sussie's mother just shook her head slowly. "You had better get home and have a bath. You stink!"

Sussie didn't argue. She ran home and enjoyed a nice warm bath, thinking how lucky she was not to be in trouble. Realizing how dangerous their game had been, Sussie never sailed a wooden shoe boat in the creek again.

* * * * *

Fall turned into winter and then winter into the spring of 1940. Sussie and Kees were attending school during the day but

Gerard wasn't old enough for school yet and stayed home with his mother. For Sussie and Kees, this was a fairly normal time of school work, playing games such as marbles in the school yard, and the usual exchange of verbal insults with the Catholic kids from school in the middle of town, which was common between the Protestant and Catholic children in the Netherlands and elsewhere in those days. Sussie loved going to school and learning new things. She had many questions and enjoyed feeding her active imagination.

"What did you do for fun when you were young?" Sussie asked her father during breakfast one Saturday morning.

Willem finished his mouthful of bacon and eggs and replied, "When it was spring like this, we would collect birds' eggs and see how many different kinds we could find. After we finish breakfast, we'll go outside and I'll show you what I mean."

A few minutes later, Sussie and her brothers followed their father outside. Willem pointed up into a large tree and said to Kees, "See that nest up there? You have to climb up there and see if there are any eggs in it. If there are, you only take one egg because we want the other eggs to hatch into baby birds. Then very carefully, carry that one egg down to the ground."

"What do I do with it once I get it down?" Kees wondered.

"You go and borrow a needle from Mom and very carefully make a little hole in each end of the egg. Then you put one end up to your mouth and gently blow out all the insides." Willem made a motion as though he was blowing the egg out himself. The look on Gerard's face suggested a feeling of disgust at the thought of doing that but, under Willem's instructions, all three children soon mastered the art of blowing out eggs. Sussie and her brothers went on to become the best bird nesters in the town of Rossum.

Against the wishes of her father, who had forbidden her to climb trees, Sussie earned her place as an expert tree climber as well. The rambunctious six year old simply climbed the trees when her father wasn't watching.

For the Cretiers, a common evening meal began with porridge and syrup. For fun, the children loved to write words on their porridge with the syrup. One evening, Gerard wrote something not so nice and his father noticed.

"What did you write there?" Willem asked his son. When Gerard said the word out loud, he received a sharp clip on the back of his head. Big tears welled up in Gerard's eyes and began to roll down his cheeks.

"You can stop crying right now and promise you won't do that again!" Willem told him sternly. Kees and Sussie started to giggle.

"You can stop the laughing or you'll get one, too!" Willem said to the others. Their meal continued in silence.

Throughout the previous year, the Netherlands had been living in the shadow of war as Germany invaded Eastern Europe. Country after country had fallen to Adolf Hitler's war machine. The Dutch government had indicated its desire to remain neutral as it had done during the First World War, and it seemed as though Germany was going to respect that wish. One evening in April 1940, with the news of war all around them, the Cretiers began to wonder.

"Have you heard anything about the war, Willem?" Geert asked her husband.

Willem didn't want to frighten the children, so he replied, "Not much. The Germans said they would honour our neutrality." Later that night, he told Geert the truth of what he had heard.

"There's talk that the Germans will invade us," Willem said after Kees, Sussie and Gerard were in bed. Although he spoke quietly, Geert could hear the concern in his voice.

"But Hitler promised he wouldn't harm us," she said, fear beginning to overtake her.

"I know," Willem replied, "but the Dutch Army is on alert and ready to fight. The Germans have such a formidable military force. I can't see us being able to keep them out."

Willem took Geert in his arms and for the next few minutes, they held each other close and prayed for a way to bring their family through the time to come. "We've started a resistance organization already," Willem continued. "We have to be ready if the Nazis take over. You know me. I can't stand by and do nothing. I have to do what I can for you and our country." His heart was heavy with the thought of placing his loved ones in danger, but his will to do what was right was also strong.

Geert nodded slowly, a tear rolling down her cheek. Whatever Willem decided to do, she would do as well.

The spring of 1940 was fading into summer and the blossoms were gone from the trees when Sussie contracted scarlet fever. Her mother knew that Sussie must be very sick. It just wasn't like her busy little daughter to lie in bed and let the world go by without investigating every occurrence. Although Sussie had fallen prey to a very serious and life-threatening disease, it turned out that the scarlet fever probably saved her life.

The Germans attacked the Netherlands at 4:00 a.m. on May 10, 1940. If Sussie had not been so sick, her inquisitive nature might have led her into considerable danger. Instead, she lay there listening to the ominous sound of gunfire, bombs exploding and war planes flying over their home. Those terrible sounds filled her with a feeling of helplessness and fear that she had never known before.

CHAPTER TWO

The invasion

"Where's Dad going?" Sussie asked her mother after Willem had come in, wearing his Army uniform, to kiss her goodbye. The scarlet fever still had Sussie in its sickly grasp, keeping her bedridden, but she was not sick enough to ignore the sounds of war or notice that her father was leaving in uniform.

Geert took her daughter in her arms. "He has to go away to be in the Army for awhile," she said.

"Is he coming back? Will he be alright?" Sussie questioned.

Geert assured Sussie that Willem wouldn't be away long and that, "Yes, he'll be just fine."

In her own heart, however, Geert was very concerned for her husband's safety, but she didn't want Sussie and her brothers to worry. Geert and Willem had resolved to keep the worst of what lay ahead to themselves, so their children would not grow up with emotional scars that could devastate their happiness. The children never learned the entire story of their parents' involvement in the Dutch war effort. They only knew what they saw or overheard, and the little bits that their parents told them about many years later.

The Netherlands was completely taken aback by the Germans' attack. Adolf Hitler had promised only the day before that he would never invade their country. "The Dutch are our friends," he boldly announced. "We are of the same blood line."

On May 13, 1940, just three days after the invasion, Queen Wilhelmina decided it would be best if she left her beloved homeland to avoid being used as a Nazi puppet. She declared that Hitler was "the arch-enemy of mankind" and she, her family and some government officials escaped to England on the British warship HMS Heerewaarden.

The Dutch Army fought bravely but was no match for the German war machine. After only five days of fighting, Hitler decided to end the invasion quickly with a strong message that could not be ignored. He ordered the German air force, the Luftwaffe, to bomb the city of Rotterdam. Almost 1,000 people were killed, many of them children trapped in their schools. Thousands more were wounded and 78,000 were left homeless. When the city of Utrecht was also threatened, the Dutch authorities surrendered to avoid further bloodshed.

Many Dutch soldiers were killed in that initial onslaught. Fortunately for Sussie and her brothers, Willem survived. He and his fellow captured soldiers were not held as prisoners of war, though. They were allowed to return to their homes. This gesture was intended as a symbol of brotherhood by the German invaders. Besides, the Germans had other plans for this hard-working group of people.

For the Cretier children, the first few days of German occupation caused fear, helplessness and emotional turmoil. Sussie was still ill in bed, but the school was closed and all the children now had to stay indoors, wondering what was happening to their beautiful country and their happy lives in Rossum. The Cretier children were grateful, however, to have their father home, knowing that thousands of other children had already lost their fathers in the war.

From Queen Wilhelmina's command post in exile, she and her officials communicated with the Dutch people through daily radio broadcasts of the British Broadcasting Corporation. A few bars of Beethoven's Fifth Symphony always preceded these important messages, a sign to her people that she would soon be speaking to them.

Another method the Queen of the Netherlands used to keep lines of communication open with her subjects was through pamphlets and posters dropped from the air and distributed by a network of Dutch patriots willing to risk their lives to get this encouraging information to the people. Willem and Geert Cretier were just two of this important organization later to be known as The Dutch Resistance.

On May 26, 1940, the Netherlands was placed under a German civil government headed by an Austrian Nazi Party official, Arthur Seyss-Inquart. "Germany does not want to annex Holland or force German ideology on the people of this country," he announced in his first speech to the nation. "Dutch laws will remain in force until further notice."

Willem and Geert listened to this broadcast with disbelief. They knew their lives would never be the same. They had heard rumours of the atrocities committed by the Germans in Poland and they were sure there had to be some truth to those horrible stories.

"They lied to us before. Why would they be telling the truth now?" Willem said in disgust.

"I just hope and pray that the terrible things we've heard about don't happen here," Geert said, fearful of what would become of her wonderful little family.

"Is there anything we can do?" she asked Willem.

"Nothing for the moment," he replied. "We will have to wait and see how this is all going to turn out. I'm sure the alliance of our people will be in touch with ways to bring our oppression to an end."

It would be some time before the Cretiers heard from the Resistance, though. A lot of organizing had to be done. When the time was right, Willem and Geert knew they would be ready to do whatever was required of them to help restore their country's freedom.

The Germans quickly took over the leadership of the Netherlands and began recruiting sympathizers to take up key political and civil positions. Many of these replacements were members of the Dutch Nazi Party, (NSB[2]), a largely despised organization that had been previously outlawed in the Netherlands. Now this group resurfaced with the boastful intention of governing the country. They felt they would be all-powerful now that Germany had taken control. In the evenings, these Nazi-wannabes marched through the streets, handing out pamphlets and encouraging others to join their organization.

"You will have a nice black uniform with white shirt and red tie! And you will have more power, and food for your family," they shouted as they marched along.

As Sussie lay in her bed trying to overcome her illness, the ominous 'clomp clomp clomp' of hobnail boots marching in the streets and the awful shouting outside their home often led her to bury her head under her pillow. "How could this be happening?" she wondered. Even at age six, she felt the anxiety and worry. She wondered what the future would bring with the Germans running their country.

Life under German rule would have been impossible without the comforting words of her mother. "Everything will be all right, Sussie. Our family is together and that will always be our strength. As long as we stay together, nothing can harm us," Geert told her.

By the end of that summer, Sussie had made a full recovery from her near-fatal bout of scarlet fever, but the summer had passed so slowly. School resumed in the fall but everything seemed strange now. The fun and laughter was gone from the children of Rossum as if some life-giving part had been taken from their very souls. The question on the minds of all the children and adults alike was, 'How long will this unwanted intrusion last?'

"Is this the home of Willem Cretier?" a well-dressed German officer asked loudly one morning as he knocked on their door.

---

[2]The National Socialist Movement in the Netherlands (Dutch: Nationaal-Socialistische Beweging in Nederland, NSB) was a Dutch fascist and later national socialist political party (www.wikipedia.org)

Having German soldiers come to your home was not Geert's idea of a good thing. She carefully opened the door. "Yes it is," she replied, peering out at this formidable visitor.

The officer forced his way inside. "I have to speak with him now," the officer barked.

Willem was seated at the table having breakfast.

"You will stand in the presence of a German officer!" the officer snarled. Willem, more than a little apprehensive, rose slowly to his feet, wondering what this was all about.

"I am informed that you are the mechanic that operates the garage here. Is that true?" questioned the officer.

"Yes, that is true," answered Willem. The officer handed him some papers.

"You have been chosen to drive the taxi in this town of Rossum for the express purpose of transporting the sick to hospital. These papers are your driving permit. You will carry them with you at all times. If you are caught driving without your permit, you will be arrested. You have been selected for this task because of your mechanical knowledge and your ability to keep the taxi running. You will be on call 24 hours a day and will respond quickly to all calls."

Willem looked down at the papers in his hand.

'I don't want to work for the Germans,' he thought as he pondered this new challenge, 'but maybe the privilege could be used for other things.'

"All right, I will do it," he said solemnly.

"Good!" said the officer. "We will be watching you." He then gave the Nazi salute, "Heil Hitler!" and left the Cretier home.

This development bothered Geert a great deal, but she waited for the German to leave before she spoke. "How are we going to do this?" she asked Willem. "You hate these monsters! Why would you want to work for them?"

"I don't want to work for them, but think about it," Willem replied. "I will have the freedom to drive here and there. Maybe there are other things I could use the taxi for," he said with a slight smile.

Geert then understood the reason behind his acceptance. She admired this man she loved for his bravery, knowing the dangers that could be ahead. She knew that some of the people who appeared to have joined the Nazis were actually members of the Dutch Resistance. They were spies, pretending to be supportive of the Nazis while passing on valuable information to the Resistance. They were at greater risk than most. They were traitors in the eyes of some of their own people but they also faced certain death if discovered by the SS[3]. Willem had no desire to join the NSB, and he never did, but he also knew that his new driving permit could have been construed as helping the Germans.

---

[3]SS – The Schutzstaffell is German for Protective Echelon and was a major political and military organization under Adolf Hitler and the Nazi Party, responsible for most of the worst crimes against humanity perpetrated by the Nazis during the Second World War. (www.wikipedia.org and www.feldgrau.com)

CHAPTER THREE

Occupation

Radical changes in the Dutch way of life continued. Food rationing was imposed. Each family was given food stamps based on what the German authorities thought would fill their needs. This was usually inadequate, though. Small-town residents like the Cretiers were more fortunate than their city counterparts because they could supplement their rations with milk and vegetables obtained from local farms. The Dutch people living in the big cities like Amsterdam and Utrecht were not as lucky. A black market for food soon established itself. Food items not available in the rations were sold for outrageous prices and, as is common in these situations, the poorest people suffered the most.

By January 1941, all British and American movies had been taken out of the theatres and replaced with German-made movies. That would not have been so bad if there had not been Nazi newsreels shown with each movie. The Dutch patrons began to boo these hated newsreels and many displayed their disgust by walking out of the theatres. This prompted the Nazi leader Seyss-Inquart to issue a decree prohibiting such behaviour. He declared that anyone caught in the act of leaving a theatre during the playing of a newsreel would be arrested. Attendance at the movies dwindled to almost nothing.

The demeaning decree also included the prohibition of listening to foreign radio stations. All Dutch radio stations had been taken over by the Germans for the express purpose of spreading Nazi propaganda. Willem and Geert secretly listened to Queen Wilhelmina's speeches of encouragement on the BBC, as did many others. They were determined that no illegitimate Nazi regime would keep the truth from them.

To the Cretiers, it seemed as though the invaders made a new demand every second day. Somewhere in the middle of March 1941, the first of many flyers was delivered to every home ordering everyone to attend a parade of the NSB and the SS. The intent was for Dutch citizens to witness the greatness of the Third Reich, the common term for Nazi Germany under Hitler's rule. Although Willem and Geert wanted nothing to do with this evil regime, they made sure they were all at the parade to avoid drawing attention to their family.

The parade was a display of German power that included bound and shackled prisoners being brutally dragged along and beaten. These prisoners' crimes were often nothing more than listening to a British radio broadcast. The gruesome parade was an ominous message to those watching of what would happen to them if they didn't comply with the new order. At one of these frequent displays of brutality, a young Dutch man spat at the German soldiers. He was quickly taken from the crowd and viciously beaten and kicked until, lying unconscious in a pool of his own blood, he was left for dead by his attackers. The same treatment was meted out on another young man who made a comment that offended the marchers.

Sussie's parents had been doing their best to protect their children from the horrors of war, but they could not keep them from viewing these cruelties. These were terrible scenes for children to witness and left indelible scars in the memories of Kees, Sussie and Gerard.

"Don't let on that you are upset, and don't get involved with any of these things," Geert warned her three children as they witnessed these brutal sideshows. "You have to remain calm, no matter what."

Sussie knew that her mother would never say these things unless the situation was very serious. Sussie wanted to help the people who were being tortured by these monsters, but she respected her mother's wishes and stayed in one spot.

It was even harder for the Dutch people to watch these displays of torture while knowing that most of the young Dutchmen, who had joined the NSB and SS and were the perpetrators of these evil deeds, had been in trouble with the Dutch police themselves before the German invasion. It wasn't easy for good people like the Cretiers to be subservient to those who were little more than criminals themselves.

Other Nazi decrees had a much more sinister undertone for the Dutch citizens. "All Jews will henceforth wear a yellow star. No Jew will be permitted to own or operate a business. All Jews who hold positions in the public service sector will be replaced."

Harassment of Jewish people by the NSB began, sparking an altercation that led to the death of a young NSB member in Amsterdam. In retaliation, the Germans arrested several hundred Dutch Jews and sent them to concentration camps. None survived.

This blatant reversal of the promise of no Nazi doctrine infuriated the residents of the Netherlands. Thousands of Dutch people began to gather in the streets to protest this latest development. They organized a national general strike.

The strike took the Germans by surprise. Nothing like this had happened in any other country that they had occupied. The Germans ordered a 7:30 p.m. curfew and brought in many more police and soldiers to deal with the situation. An official announcement was made. "Anyone not returning to work immediately will be fined or fired!"

Only municipal workers returned to work, however. Martial law was declared. Heavily armed German police and Gestapo[4] units patrolled the streets and many Dutch people

[4]Gestapo – Nazi political police

were killed. The instigators of the strike were hunted down and about 100 of them were arrested and sent to concentration camps, never to return. The strike was broken but the Germans knew now that while they might control the country of the Netherlands, they could never control the hearts of its stalwart people.

Tighter controls were imposed. Rations were cut further. All young Dutchmen were ordered to report for work in Germany to support the German war machine. Many went into hiding and joined the Resistance movement. The noose was tightening on the people of the Netherlands and the actions of the Underground became more intense. They began to sabotage German operations, started their own secret newspaper, developed code names for each other and generally created as much havoc as they could for their oppressors.

Many different people visited the Cretier home during this time, one of whom was Pastor Daniels. He visited frequently and Sussie thought this was strange since he wasn't the minister for their church. He seemed like a happy man, though. He had a twinkle in his eyes and always brought candy for the children, which Sussie and her brothers appreciated. More importantly, Tommy liked Pastor Daniels and if that big dog liked him, then the pastor must be a good person, Sussie thought.

The children always heard Pastor Daniels coming long before he arrived because his robe made a swishing sound like that of running water. Every time he came to visit, Geert asked Sussie, Kees and Gerard to play outside or do an errand for her. Many years later, the children learned that Pastor Daniels was an integral part of the Dutch Resistance and needed time alone with Willem and Geert to discuss Underground business.

A while later, another encroachment on the Dutch people's freedom was announced. "All radios will be turned in at a central collection point. It is against the law to have one in your possession."

Willem took in his large old radio as ordered, hoping that the Germans would accept this as an indication of his subservience, but it appeared that they needed more evidence to substantiate his innocence. A thorough search of the Cretier home followed but failed to find the smaller, better radio hidden up in a small niche inside the chimney. Along with the small radio, Willem had also hidden his pistol and the Dutch/English dictionary he needed to translate messages to and from the Allies. Any one of these items uncovered would have meant certain death for Willem and his family.

"What is that sound I can hear late at night while I'm lying in bed?" Sussie asked her mother one morning.

"What sound do you hear?" Geert asked her.

"I hear something like deep music. It kind of goes, ba ba ba boom ba ba ba boom." Without knowing the actual tune, Sussie was reciting the first few bars of Beethoven's Fifth Symphony.

"I don't know of any sound like that," Geert lied to her daughter. "Are you sure you weren't dreaming?"

Sussie was adamant. "No, I was not dreaming! I was wide awake! Some nights, I hear that sound and other nights, nothing."

"Well, I don't know what that could be, but I will ask your father and see what he says," Geert assured her daughter.

Sussie never heard the music again after that morning. Many years later, her parents explained what she had heard.

For Willem, the permit he had been given to drive taxi made him exempt from the evening curfew. He made good use of this privilege and secretly transported Jewish people from one safe place to another as well as Allied airmen who had been shot down over the Netherlands. If Sussie had known how much danger her father had placed himself in almost every night, she likely would not have slept a wink during the entire war. To be caught aiding the Allies or Jewish people would mean certain death.

Gathering information on German military positions for the Allies was another of Willem's covert activities. He took mental notes of all their movements during the course of his taxi obligations and passed the information on to other Underground members who, in turn, passed it on to the Allies.

Sussie's daily experiences changed considerably during this time. With no unauthorized civilians allowed on the streets at night after curfew, the only thing heard was the ominous sound of marching hobnailed boots and those awful German military songs that Sussie had grown to hate. Daytime wasn't much more fun either.

Sussie's parents had warned their children not to speak to anyone outside of their own family and never to talk about anything that was discussed at home. This warning led Sussie and her brothers to avoid some people as much as possible. They were especially on their guard whenever the local policeman was around. He seemed really sneaky to them and they didn't think he could be trusted. Sussie felt the same way about a local farmer.

He was a large jovial man who often tried to win her confidence by talking to her and her brothers. Sometimes, he would talk to Sussie when she was alone. He made her feel very uneasy.

"So what have you been doing today?" he asked.

"Nothing. Just playing," Sussie said coyly.

"So how do you feel about what's happening with the Germans here?" the farmer queried.

"I don't know," Sussie answered, shrugging her shoulders.

The farmer pressed harder for information. "Does your Daddy ever talk to you about the Germans?"

"No, we never talk about that," she said, feeling like it was time to end the conversation. "I've got to go and find my brothers now." Then she ran off.

Almost a year had passed since the invasion and Sussie was tired of the tension and lack of fun in her life. She had some comforting distractions with Tommy at times. The big, gentle pet was a great swimmer and he acted as the children's lifeguard when they went swimming in the Waal River. The children were able to go to school again but it was never the same as before.

Sussie soon began to feel like a prisoner in her own home. All the fun times she and her brothers had had with their friends in Rossum were now a thing of the past. It was no longer safe to go anywhere without their mother or father. Sussie wanted to go outside and play with her brothers and her friends, but Geert suggested that the children only play in their own yard. German soldiers, NSB members and the dreaded Gestapo were everywhere. Not to mention some of the neighbours who spied on everything they did and reported to the Nazis.

Willem and Geert did their best to maintain a happy atmosphere in their home. Saturday evenings provided some of the best memories for Sussie. Her father would bring home a big bag of peanuts which were placed in a large bowl in the middle of the kitchen table along with the latest newspaper. A discussion of the week's events ensued, including talk of personal events that each of them had experienced during the week as well as the newspaper articles. These nights were welcome respites from the horrors outside their front door.

Over the next year, the Germans somewhat relaxed their hard-line rule and life seemed almost normal for a few months. In fact, the Cretiers made friends with a German soldier in his late 30s that visited their home occasionally. Willem and Geert sensed he was a good man and Geert made a pot of tea for him when he dropped by. During one of these visits, the soldier said that Sussie reminded him of his own daughter who was about the same age and that he missed being with his family.

Then Sussie asked, "Do you like this war?"

Geert endured the ensuing strained silence with fearful anticipation. Would this end their friendship? Would their visitor be offended? Or worse, would he inform the SS?

Willem and the boys were out at the time, so the outcome of this moment would be shared only between the three of them.

After a few more anxious seconds, a look of sadness entered the soldier's eyes as he slowly shook his head and answered, "No."

The silence returned. Geert wondered how to change the subject and Sussie felt compassion for this man and his honesty. Geert spoke first. "Would you like some more tea?" she asked.

"Yes, thank you," he replied. "That would be nice." The ice had been broken and the tense moment alleviated. The small talk resumed.

The soldier never visited again and the Cretiers often wondered what had happened to him. He was too nice to be a part of Hitler's plan.

School holidays began in December 1942 with nothing specific for the children to do, but they kept themselves entertained in any way they could. Geert saw her children sliding down the dyke one day on a large wooden shoe that they had found. The children had taken the top off the shoe to create a great toboggan for themselves. All they needed was a little water on the slope of the dyke and then they took turns sitting on the shoe and letting gravity take them very quickly to the bottom. The children loved this game of sliding down a steep 10-metre slope, but their mother was concerned for their safety, especially that of her only daughter.

"Sussie, why don't you play with your dolls like other girls do?" Geert asked her daughter after she had come inside with mud all over her clothes from the dyke-sliding escapade.

"Oh, I don't know. I have more fun playing with my brothers, I guess," Sussie answered.

Geert made her fears known to Willem and he quickly assured his wife that he would find something else for the children to do during the holidays. He gave them the task of taking apart an old car. "That will keep them out of mischief for most of the school break," Willem said to Geert. But the Cretiers underestimated their children and were surprised when the job was finished after only three days.

"You can't be finished already," exclaimed Willem when the three budding mechanics told him the job was done. He went to check on their work and found that all the bolts were in the boxes and the car parts were all stacked neatly. He couldn't help but marvel at how quickly they had performed what he considered to be a difficult and time-consuming task. 'Well, I guess I proved one thing,' he thought. 'I've got three smart kids!'

Early in 1943, Seyss-Inquart issued another decree. This time, he outlawed the display of either the Dutch national flag or the Orange flag, the symbol of the Dutch Royal family. Prince Bernhard's birthday was June 29 and, despite the Nazi orders, the Dutch people continued their tradition of wearing little orange carnations in their lapels to honour their prince. The Germans were furious at this and considered it an act of defiance to honour a man they considered a traitor, a German Royal who had married a Dutch princess. Still, there was very little they could do about this display because there were too many offenders to incarcerate them all. This widespread act of insubordination showed the Nazis that the majority of the Dutch people did not support their occupation and would continue to support their own Royal family in spite of the Germans' presence.

It was around this time that clothing and other consumer goods became even scarcer. Geert couldn't find the things she needed for her children in Rossum and decided to take them on a bus trip to nearby Hertogenbosch, a larger city to the south of Rossum. The supplies there turned out to be not much better than in Rossum, but at least it was a day out for Geert and her children.

Geert decided to treat eight-year-old Sussie and her brothers to some ice cream that day. They were seated by the restaurant window, enjoying their ice cream, when a large group of German soldiers marched into view singing a military song.

"Look, Mom," said young Gerard in a loud voice. "Look how many rotten Germans there are out there!"

Geert felt like her heart had stopped. A group of German officers was seated at the table next to them, having a meal. 'Had they heard Gerard?' she wondered in alarm.

Sussie recognized the danger and quickly took matters into her own hands. "Hey, Kees!" she yelled at her older brother, "What did you do that for?"

Kees immediately caught on to Sussie's ploy.

"I didn't do anything!" he yelled back at his sister.

"Mom! Stop him from being mean to me," Sussie yelled, deliberately escalating the altercation. Just as Sussie intended, their loud argument took the attention off her little brother.

"Come on, children. Stop the fighting! We have to go and catch the bus," Geert said. They left the restaurant as quickly as they could to get to safety.

"That was quick thinking, Sussie," Geert later said to her daughter. Geert silently resolved never to go to Hertogenbosch again, at least until after the war was over.

Despite the terror, subterfuge and oppression of this era, there were moments of happiness for the Cretier children when their grandmother came to visit. Sussie felt that her Oma made the best sausages in the world and they all looked forward to the times when she would come to their house to make smoked sausages. The children tried to help wherever they could and after the sausages were made, they all sat down to a tasty meal. Unfortunately, these brief respites with Oma were few and far between.

Oma's sausage also served a secondary purpose, in convincing the children's dog to become a perfect sled dog. When Sussie and her brothers first harnessed the big beast to the snow sled their father had built, Tommy wasn't sure of his new job. So Sussie suggested they get some of their Oma's sausage and hang it on a stick in front of Tommy. "He likes it so much, I'll bet he'll chase it," Sussie said. The sausage did the trick and every time after that when the sled was brought out of the shed, Tommy became excited, knowing that after he had given the children a fun time sledding, he would be given some of the sausage for a treat.

On April 29, 1943, the Germans rescinded another promise. They ordered all Dutch Army veterans to report for interment in Germany. This sparked a wildcat strike beginning at an armaments factory in Hengelo. The workers simply put down their tools and walked out. Word of the strike spread quickly throughout the country. Within hours, more than 500,000 workers from industrial to agricultural sectors had withdrawn their labour. This, like the first strike, took the Germans by surprise. An order was issued that all workers must return to work and not be involved in demonstrations. Failure to comply would bring severe penalties. More than 80 men thought to have been instigators of the strike were publicly executed by firing squad.

It seemed as though this succession of infringements on the freedom of the Dutch people would never end. The Germans started conducting surprise searches of Dutch homes, taking anything of value they could find. Willem and Geert buried some of their valuables along with their silverware in their back yard, as did many of their neighbours. Bicycles were confiscated and sent to Germany. Anything made of brass or copper was taken. Photographs were confiscated and destroyed. It wasn't clear to the Dutch people why their pictures were being taken, but many people had difficulty giving up their captured moments in time. It was later revealed that the Nazis were trying to eradicate any record of the existence of Dutch Jews, and photographs were targeted as reminders that needed to be demolished.

The Dutch people were asked for fiscal contributions to assist with the German war effort. This last request was denied by almost every Dutch citizen. "They have nerve asking us for money!" Willem said in disgust one day, echoing the feelings of most of his countrymen. "They make it harder and harder for us to earn a living and then ask us for money! Never!"

Rationing was cut again in an attempt to bring out those in hiding or at least give an indication of where they were hiding, by watching for those who sought extra food. Even soap was hard to obtain. Geert began making her own soap out of chestnuts. It was very slippery and it took the family some time to adapt to this new soap. Clothes were impossible to buy. Worn clothes were cut down into smaller ones to eliminate the worn-out areas. Fabric for patching eventually ran out as well. Clothes were worn until they literally fell off the wearer.

The Dutch people reverted to wearing the age-old wooden clogs that their ancestors had worn more than a hundred years earlier because leather shoes were no longer available. School children had difficulty identifying whose clogs were whose and started painting designs and names on them to alleviate this problem. For young Sussie, the clumping sound made by all those wooden shoes on the sidewalks at the end of a school day made her giggle.

Every time the Germans stepped up their attempts to flush out those in hiding, the Resistance stepped up its efforts to thwart them. Nighttime raids were conducted on the offices that distributed ration cards and the cards obtained were given to families in need or to those giving safe harbour to fugitives. Willem was heavily involved in these dangerous activities and his permit to drive the taxi was put to good use during this time.

As 1944 began, the Germans started gathering up the Jews and sending them in cattle cars to concentration camps, another promise broken and a terrible blow for Willem and Geert. A good friend of theirs, Ies Stranders, his young wife and little daughter were among the first to go. Their son Louis was only a baby at the time and was kept hidden from the Nazis. (He survived the war and made his home in Zaltbommel.)

The Gestapo came to the Rossum school one day and took all the Jewish children away. These were friends of Sussie and her brothers. The Cretiers didn't know where their friends were being taken at the time, but had an awful feeling that this was not a good development. Jewish families who went into hiding to avoid this terrible turn of events were split up and sent to safe houses to avoid being captured. Before the war was over, more than 100,000 Dutch Jews perished in the Holocaust.

A young Jewish girl named Chell Hes was brought to the Cretier home to be hidden from the Germans. The Cretiers told everyone her name was Sjaantje Heestra (pronounced Shonjee), she was from The Hague and her family had no food so the Cretiers were going to look after her for awhile. The Cretiers did not have much for themselves, but Geert and Willem never refused an opportunity to help others and immediately agreed to shelter this young girl for as long as it was safe to do so.

Geert told Sussie and her brothers the same story when introducing this new member of their family. "This is Sjaantje. She will go to school with you and live here as one of our family." Sjaantje was the same age as Kees and they got along well from the beginning, playing together and going to school in the same class.

Sjaantje soon discovered how much fun it was to be towed through the snow on a sled behind Tommy. It became her favourite pastime during her stay with Sussie's family. She took part in every activity with the Cretiers, including attending Sunday school, even though she was not Christian. Outward appearances had to show that she was not Jewish.

Willem's partner in the bus company and his son were arrested when the Germans learned of his links to the Underground and involvement in a sabotage operation. A search of the partner's house revealed a radio and other materials associated with the Resistance. This was a devastating blow to Willem and he went, at the risk of his own safety, to the officer in charge of the Rossum area to plead for his friend.

"You are too late," the German told him. "They are already on their way to the concentration camp in Neuengamme. If you are a friend of theirs, then you are a suspect, too. So don't let me catch you doing anything against us. Do you understand?" Willem assured the officer that he understood and he left the office feeling empty and defeated. Word came a few weeks later that Willem's partner and his son had died from repeated beatings, starvation and dysentery. The news of these deaths was a sickening blow to Willem, but strengthened his resolve to do all he could to end this nightmare of Nazi reign.

Sjaantje was only with the Cretiers for a few weeks when people in the community began asking too many questions.

"Who is this girl?"

"Where did she come from?"

"I think she is Jewish," one woman said to Geert. "We have been watching her and she is not like us. I don't think she is from The Hague. I am sure she is a Jew."

Geert, able to keep calm in every situation, gently replied. "How can you say that? She is a lovely girl and we love her like our very own. She can't help it if her family can't afford to feed her."

One evening, Sussie's grandmother came to visit. "Who is this little girl you have living with you?" she asked. "You know how it will be for you if she is found out to be Jewish. I am the last one to wish her any harm, but people are asking questions. You will have to make up your mind very quickly now. The Germans are sure to come and see what she is all about."

Geert said, "If that is true, then I will find another place for her."

Locating a new safe home for Sjaantje wasn't an easy task, however. People were afraid to help for fear of being shot by the Nazis but finally, another safe house was found for Sjaantje. The night she was taken there was a sad one for Sussie, Kees and Gerard because she had become a good friend to them during her stay. Sussie's whole family was crying, including

Willem. They all hugged Sjaantje and wished her safe passage, not knowing if they would ever see her again.

Sjaantje and her family, scattered in safe houses throughout the Netherlands, survived the war thanks to the bravery of those who sheltered them. The Hes family moved to Israel after the war and Chell (Sjaantje) planted a tree in a grove there as a symbol of thanks to the Cretier family for helping save her life.

At about the time that Sjaantje left them, the Cretier children lost another close companion. Tommy became ill and the local veterinarian told them that the big strong dog had a terminal illness and could not be restored to health. Telling the children that he had to put down this caring pet was difficult for Willem, especially when they had already witnessed so much pain from the war.

"We'll get another puppy," he promised his distraught daughter. "I know it is hard to let go of a pet that has meant so much to you, but he will always be with you in your heart."

Willem kept his word and soon brought home a cute puppy. This was Atoz, a German hunting dog. Atoz turned out to be a loving and protective dog and soon took his place as a member of the Cretier family. Sussie loved this dog, too, but never really forgot her beloved Tommy.

* * * * *

"I just got some good news," Willem said to Geert one day in June 1944. "The Allies have landed a massive invasion in Normandy and they are coming our way. We are going to be free!"

A feeling of jubilation swept through the Netherlands and many took to the streets in celebration. Geert felt hope for the first time in four years. It would be the end of this nightmare. It was almost too much to believe.

Their hopes were dashed as the invasion stalled. The Allies had landed in the Netherlands but the fight to liberate their country would take far longer than anticipated. A secondary invasion of paratroopers called 'Market Garden' was a complete failure, resulting in the death of most of the Allied soldiers who participated in it. The weather didn't help either. Rain, rain and more rain made an already damp countryside almost impossible to negotiate. Mud became the Allied soldiers' constant companion and enemy.

Only after some terrible battles with heavy casualties did Canadian Forces liberate much of the southern part of the Netherlands. By the end of summer, some of the Canadian Forces made it to the Maas River, not far from Rossum. This was to be as far as they would advance for several months. But they were so close now. Just over the river. Willem became even busier supplying the Canadians with information on German military positions.

The tide was turning against their captors. Every night, many Allied bombers crossed over the Cretiers' land on their way to bomb Germany. The Nazis had ordered that all windows be blacked out so that no light shone through and gave Allied pilots a beacon to guide them to Germany. If any small glimmer of light showed from a house window, the Germans were soon banging on the door of that house and imposing an immediate fine.

Remembering the first time she had heard many airplanes at night when the Germans attacked their country, Sussie listened to the incessant drone with a very different emotion now. It wasn't fear that filled her heart this time. It was hope. This was the sound of Allied Forces attacking Germany! She and all her country had been waiting for this! To be liberated from the terror of life under Nazi rule. Yes, the sound of these bombers gave her hope. Hope of freedom and a return to a normal life!

Sussie's father was away from home almost every night now. Many Allied bombers were shot down by German anti-aircraft fire. Rescuing the crews was a major priority for the Dutch Underground. Transporting these brave airmen to safety was extremely difficult due to the topography of the Netherlands. There were no forests or mountains in which to hide and there were many rivers with bridges. This made it easy for the Germans to keep tight controls on the movement of people.

Despite these adversities, Willem was still able to save many Allied airmen from capture and return them to their own lines by using his permit to drive the taxi and his connections in the Dutch Underground network. Willem knew that the freeing of his country was only a matter of time now. Liberation was so close, he could taste it.

* * * * *

One day in August 1944, Willem received a pamphlet through the Resistance network from Queen Wilhelmina. It contained a poster of the queen along with an encouraging message from her. Willem, ever loyal to his monarch, hung the queen's picture on the wall in the Cretiers' home.

"Don't you think that's a dangerous thing to do?" Geert asked. "What if a German sees it hanging there?"

"It's alright," Willem replied. "I've hung it so it can only be seen from my chair and I'm the only one who sits there."

Sussie wasn't happy with the idea of a possible confrontation with the Germans either, and told her father so.

"You worry too much," Willem said to his young daughter.

The family's fears were soon realized. A German captain came to visit Willem only a few days later. Sussie's keen instincts told her this was not good, so she immediately sat in her father's chair, to prevent the German officer from using it.

"You must go outside and play," the officer said to Sussie.

"I don't feel like playing today," Sussie answered quietly. The German seemed to accept her refusal for a moment and continued his conversation with Willem. Then he abruptly returned his attention to Sussie.

"You will move now! I want to sit down!" he said in a curt voice and forced Sussie out of her father's chair.

The moment the officer sat down, he saw the poster of Queen Wilhelmina. Immediately he rose, went to the poster and tore it off the wall.

"What is this garbage?" he screamed at Willem...

* * * * *

It seemed like hours since Sussie had saved her father's life and then gone to her favourite spot on the dyke. Thinking about those awful words again jolted her back to reality with the sting of a whiplash.

'How long have I been sitting here?' she thought. 'What time is it?' It seemed as though she had relived every day of the last four years and was still having a hard time believing what had just happened at their home.

'I'd better be getting home now. It's getting dark and Mom and Dad will be wondering where I am. I know it was wrong of me to lie but I still have my father and for that, I am truly thankful."

The Cretier house was very quiet when Sussie walked in.

"I am very tired, Mom. I think I'll just go and lie down," she said to Geert.

'A good sleep may bring a better tomorrow,' Sussie thought to herself as she got herself ready for bed.

Above: Rossum School class photo. Five-year-old Sussie Cretier is seated in the
front row, fifth from the left.

Left: Geert Cretier and Gerard, before the
German invasion, 1939.

Below: The Roman Catholic church in Rossum,
Netherlands.

CHAPTER FOUR

Bob Elliott

'Wow, this is great!' Bob Elliott thought to himself as he admired the new bike he had just purchased. He was 13 years old in the summer of 1938 and had been working hard at his part-time job as a bicycle courier for Jack's 10-Cent Delivery in Calgary. The company kept five cents from every delivery and the courier got the other five cents, and Bob had been able to save enough to buy this beautiful heavy-duty bike. Now he would have no trouble delivering the heavy loads he was required to carry.

The city of Calgary in the western Canadian province of Alberta was a great place for a young teenager to be in 1938. The Great Depression of the last decade was coming to an end and there were plenty of jobs for those who wanted to work, and Bob Elliott really wanted to work. It felt good to have money in his pockets.

Sometimes he thought about all the events that led to where he was now. Like how his mom Robina and dad William had moved the whole Elliott family from Scotland to the great plains of Alberta with their seven children in tow. John was born in 1910, Peggy in 1912 and Ruby in 1917. Bill arrived in 1914, followed by Betty in 1919, Matt in 1924 and Bob in June 1925. Then Grace was born in Canada in 1929 and Charles arrived in 1932. With all these siblings, Bob was never short of someone to play with when he was a child.

Wee Robert, as his family called him, was not yet two years old when the Elliotts immigrated to Canada in the spring of

1927, but he had memories of parts of that trip including the unloading and loading of large trunks onto the trains heading west. The family put all their belongings on a truck when they arrived in Alberta. The truck promptly got stuck in the mud while travelling to their new home on a farm about nine miles northwest of Olds, Alberta. Although Bob never actually lived in the town of Olds, that town would later become significant in his life.

A farmer driving a big tractor pulled that truck out of the mud on the Elliotts' first day in Alberta. In the irony of rural life, the man driving the tractor was Jack Stirton, who later married Bob's sister Peggy.

One of Bob's favourite childhood memories occurred when he was four years old. His oldest brother John put Bob in a suitcase and carried him to the gate of their farm. John was pretending to take Wee Robert with him to the central United States where John worked during harvest every summer and made good wages for his efforts. This antic was fun for Bob, who would have done anything to stay in that suitcase and go along with his beloved older brother.

Bob looked forward to the days when John came home from his American trips. John always had chocolate bars stowed away in his suitcase for his younger brothers and sisters, which were a real treat to kids on the farm. The stories John told of his travels fascinated Bob, too. Bob often suggested that his brother should write a book about his adventures some day, but that did not come to pass.

As a boy on the farm, Bob had more than his own share of escapades. When he was about nine years old, he was riding on the platform behind the seed drill while his dad was driving the tractor. Bob's job was to move the machine's lever to lift the drill up and down at the appropriate moment to start and stop the seeding process.

When the tractor was turning a corner one time, Bob looked down at all the little cogs that regulated the seed and noticed that some of them were no longer turning. This was only because the entire rig was turning a corner and the cogs were supposed to stop at that point, but Bob did not know this. So he stuck the index finger of his right hand into the stalled spot on the drill just as the cogs started to turn again. And off came the tip of Bob's finger!

Bob was scared that his father would be mad at him for doing something stupid and would punish him with 'a licking.' His father had never done that before, but Bob thought this just might be the time that he would, so Bob just stuffed his hand in his shirt pocket and hoped that his father wouldn't notice.

Bob's dad did notice a few seconds later, though. He saw the blood soaking through Bob's shirt and called back from the tractor seat, "What's wrong? How come you're bleeding?"

Bob had to confess to his mistake and he was soon on his way to Olds in their neighbour's truck. Dr. Mann sewed up Bob's injured finger and, after the pain of the first few days, Bob's injury healed well.

Not too long after that incident, young Bob decided to cut a piece of string using a large axe. Years later, Bob could not recall the reason that he needed the string to be shorter. At that moment in time, Bob only knew that the string needed to be cut and the axe was the closest cutting tool to him.

"Watch your fingers!" Bob's dad hollered, but his warning came a second too late. As the words left his father's mouth, the axe took off the end of Bob's index finger on his left hand.

So Bob travelled back to Olds to see Dr. Mann again for more of the same treatment. Now he had matching digits. The shortened fingers became a permanent reminder of his time on the farm.

A pivotal point in Bob's early life was the deterioration of his father's health, causing the Elliott family to leave the farm and move to Calgary. Bob missed farm life but learned quickly to enjoy the city, especially during the first week in July. The Calgary Stampede rodeo billed as 'The Greatest Show on Earth!' was always a great time for Bob, his four brothers and four sisters, especially when they found a way to sneak into the fair grounds without paying.

Bob missed the countryside at times and didn't particularly like being called a country bumpkin by the city kids, but city life had its advantages, including the variety of sports available. Bob loved sports and ice hockey was his favourite. What a great game, so fast and furious. Bob was a goalkeeper and loved it when his school hockey team won the provincial championship. That was a good feeling! Bob practised hockey with the Bentley brothers, who later became big stars in the National Hockey League. It was fun to skate with such talented players.

In the summertime, Bob played baseball and softball. He was pretty good at those sports as well. All in all, he led a pretty busy life as a teenager.

* * * * *

In September 1939, 14-year-old Bob was walking home from a ball game in Calgary when a stranger called out to him, "Canada has declared war on Germany and we're in it!"

Bob didn't think too much about that news until his oldest brother John came happily skipping down the street two days later with the news that he had joined the Calgary Highlanders, a division of the Royal Canadian Army. To begin his training, John had to leave his farm near Rocky Mountain House and move to Calgary.

Bob's parents weren't impressed with the news of their eldest son's enlistment, but John was 29 years old now and married with children of his own, so there was nothing they could do to stop him. What made this news even more difficult for them to hear was that they had left Scotland in part to get John away from the idea of becoming a soldier, and now he had enlisted to fight for Canada.

Not too long after John's announcement, the second oldest brother in the family also enlisted. Bill, four years younger than

John and 11 years older than Bob, signed up with the Royal Canadian Army Service Corps as a driver. He was immediately shipped to England. Bill was the first of four Elliott brothers to see action in the Second World War. John, the first to enlist, had been re-assigned and was still in training at Shilo, Manitoba.

Around this time, Bob was offered extra work by one of his delivery customers. The owner of Big Bear Meat Market noticed Bob's hard-work ethic and hired him to work on the weekends delivering directly for him. When he wasn't delivering meat, Bob learned to cut meat and make sausages for the shop.

In the summer of 1940, a building boom began in Calgary with expansion of the Army barracks in the southwest part of the city. Bob was hired as a carpenter's helper and paid 75 cents an hour. This boosted his earnings to $30 a week, which was three times what he'd been making at his delivery job. Life was now starting to look pretty rosy for this ambitious young man.

Bob graduated from Grade 9 and started Grade 10 that year, but his heart was no longer into schoolwork. Making good money from his various jobs had a lot to do with his discontented disposition. He felt that there must be more to life than sitting in a classroom for most of the day. He wanted to be working full time.

Then there were all these big posters with soldiers on them pointing a finger right at Bob, or so it felt to him as he walked by one of the signs. "WE NEED YOU!" the posters seemed to scream in large bold letters.

Bob was only 15 years old when that message got the better of him, in the winter of 1940-1941.

His parents had recently separated and living at home was not the same without his father around. Having two brothers already serving in the military also had an influence on what Bob did next. He had heard that the 78th Battery was drafting recruits, so he went to the Armoury and asked the recruiting officer, "How do I join up?"

"How old are you, son?" the officer fired back.

Bob was big for his age and looked older than his 15 years. "Twenty," Bob answered without batting an eye.

"Sign here," said the officer as he pushed some papers over his desk at Bob.

That was it.

On February 14, 1941, Bob Elliott became a Canadian soldier.

"I've joined the Army," Bob told his mother when he returned home that day.

Robina Elliott was unhappy with the idea of yet another son going off to war, especially one so young. "I don't think so," she said. "I'll soon get you out of that one."

Bob felt disappointed. He had thought his mother would be pleased that he was going to fight for the freedom of his country, and he tried to convince her to let him go.

"I'll tell you what I will do," his mom continued after thinking about her son's decision for a moment. "I'll let you go, provided you sign half of your pay over to me. I will save it for you for when you come home."

Bob's disappointment started to dissipate. "Sure, I'll sign half over to you," he said quickly, his excitement returning. And it was settled.

Bob's father William gave Bob his blessing. "I can understand how you feel, son. If I were a younger, fitter man, I would probably do the same. All I can say is, I wish you the best of luck and pray for your safe return."

The next few days were a whirlwind for Bob. He felt like he had been caught up in one of those summer tornadoes that frequent the prairies of Alberta. Three days after enlisting, he was dressed in an ill-fitting uniform and on his way to Edmonton to meet the rest of his unit of about 20 young recruits who were later assigned to the 78th Battery of the 13th Field Regiment of the Royal Canadian Army.

Bob couldn't remember all the soldiers' names but he did keep track of Johnny and Bill Underhill from Calgary; Murray, Foote and Einerson from Grande Prairie; and Kilcop and Potts from British Columbia. Like any group of young men put together in close quarters, their conversations invariably turned to their own lives before enlisting. Girlfriends and wives were among their favourite topics.

After only two days in Edmonton, the group of raw young soldiers was loaded onto a train and sent east to Winnipeg, Manitoba, where they were joined by two more Batteries – the 44th from Prince Albert, Saskatchewan, and the 22nd from Nanaimo, British Columbia. These young men from all over Western Canada soon became friends, building a comradeship that would last through the difficult times ahead.

Winnipeg. Now, that city was as cold in February as its name sounded to a 15-year-old boy! One of Bob's first duties there was standing guard in front of Osbourne Barracks with an empty rifle in -40 degrees Fahrenheit. While standing in that frozen place with an icy wind blowing right through him, Bob talked to himself over and over again.

'Bob Elliott, what have you done to yourself for $1.30 a day? You could still be in Calgary making $30 a week and be inside at night, out of the cold!'

But being the determined young man he was, after working two jobs and helping his team win hockey games, Bob vowed to dedicate himself to his new job fulfilling his duty as a soldier in the Canadian Army. Things just had to get better than this.

After only two days in Winnipeg, the troop was on the move again. This time, they were sent further east to a place called Debert, Nova Scotia. There was no town at Debert. The nearest community of any size was Truro, 13 miles to the east. This was just an Army training camp and the place where the 20 young westerners met the rest of the 13th Field Regiment and became a part of the 78th Battery.

"Where are you from?" asked the interviewing officer when Bob reached the front of the line on his first day there.

"Calgary, Alberta," Bob replied.

"Tell me about your life there before you decided to enlist."

"Well, I was working in construction, playing hockey in the winter, baseball in the summer and I played in the Calgary Boys' Band."

"Sounds like you were a busy young man," the officer continued. "What instrument did you play in that band?"

"The trumpet and the tuba," Bob answered without hesitation. It was at parade the next day when he realized he shouldn't have mentioned his ability to play the trumpet.

"Elliott!" barked the drill sergeant. "I understand that you play the trumpet."

"Yessir!" Bob answered.

"Good," the sergeant went on. "You are now the Battery bugler!"

'Oh boy,' thought Bob, 'just what I need.'

So Bob Elliott became the 78th Battery's bugler, rising every morning before everyone else to play 'Reveille' and being the last to go to bed every night after playing 'Lights Out.'

Bob had thought Winnipeg was cold in February, but it was no match for Halifax. The men in Bob's regiment took turns guarding the shore and it was the most uncomfortable feeling Bob had ever experienced. The damp wind off the Atlantic Ocean ripped through him like a giant ghostly hand, penetrating his soul. He had to keep moving to prevent his boots from freezing to the wooden dock.

'If any Germans show up here, I will gladly give them this miserable place!' Bob thought at the time. 'No decent human being should have to endure these conditions!'

Debert had only recently been designated a military training ground. It was located in an old forest that had been clear cut some years before and although all the trees had been cut down and removed, their stumps remained. After several weeks of extremely hard work, the young soldiers managed to clear out all of the old tree stumps. Their next job was to tramp down the snow to form the surface of the parade ground. After many miles of walking back and forth, that job was completed.

The serious training of these young recruits began in Debert. Bob and his comrades spent the next few months learning how to shoot various weapons from rifles to field guns. Bob preferred the big guns and he quickly became the number one gunner in his regiment, with the highest rate of accuracy using the field guns.

Kitchen and latrine duties were also part of every soldier's life, but Bob felt he had somehow been assigned to more than his fair share of these mundane tasks. 'I'm sure the sergeant hates me,' he thought as he scrubbed pots and pans and cleaned toilets on the same day. His willingness to work paid off, though, as his sergeant presented him with his first stripe and promoted him to the position of lance bombardier, which came with a 10-cent raise. Bob now earned $1.40 per day and had also landed the responsibility of being in charge of kitchen duties. Things were looking up.

The Army training in Nova Scotia was hard work for all the soldiers, filled with parade ground drill, small arms and field gun instruction. Without realizing what was happening to them, this group of young men from the Canadian West was being moulded into a formidable fighting force.

In the fall of 1941, word came down through the chain of command that someone of great importance was coming to inspect the soldiers training at Debert Barracks. Parade ground rehearsals for this event went on for three weeks prior to the event. The important guest turned out to be Princess Elizabeth, who later became Queen Elizabeth II. Her Royal Highness rode in a jeep up and down the rows of young soldiers standing at attention and was then taken to the officers' mess for refreshments. To the soldiers, this visit by the beautiful young princess was the highlight of their stay at Debert and a brief respite from their otherwise gruelling routine.

Soon after the Royal visit, an announcement was made. The 3rd Canadian Division, of which Bob's regiment was a part, was about to be shipped to England for further training. They would be a step closer to deployment in the war that was raging in Europe.

Bob immediately thought of his brothers John and Bill, who were already in England. He quickly wrote them each a letter asking if there was anything they might need. John replied, "Bring some onions. We can't buy any here. Vegetables are scarce." So Bob packed some onions among the clothes he had in his kitbag.

One of the other items he packed was a large bar of brown Army soap, the kind that he and every other Canadian soldier had been issued. While they were all packing their kits one day, a fellow soldier joked about the soap. "This is in case our ship gets sunk. We can all wash ourselves ashore!" he said. The comment brought a few momentary smiles to the faces of these young men who were marching full force into the unknown.

A 48-hour embarkation leave was given to Bob and his mates in September 1941. The soldiers were given only two days to visit their families before boarding the ship that would take them to England. Happily, the allotted time did not include travel time. It took Bob four and a half days of travelling on the train to make it back to Calgary.

He enjoyed a two-day visit with family and friends and was glad that they promised to send him letters from home. He knew that their letters would bring him great comfort during some lonely and frightening times.

All too soon, Bob was back on the train for the long ride back to Nova Scotia, but those who expected to be leaving for England immediately were disappointed. There were still several weeks of waiting before a suitable troop ship could be secured for their journey.

Finally, on November 3, 1941, the 4,500 soldiers of the 3rd Canadian Division boarded the Louis Pasteur for a trip across the Atlantic Ocean. Bob marvelled at the number of ships in the convoy. Sixty ships all sailing together. What an amazing sight for a young man from the Prairies!

Two days out of Halifax, the Louis Pasteur parted company with the convoy and sailed north. A group of German U-boats had been detected, apparently waiting to sink as many of these ships as possible. The fleet commander decided it would be wise to split the convoy into smaller groups, minimizing the chances of being sunk by the torpedoes waiting in the launching tubes of those deadly submarines.

By the time Bob became a passenger on the Louis Pasteur, the old ship was no longer the luxury cruise liner it had once been. The plumbing, for instance, left a lot to be desired. Temporary toilets designed to accommodate thousands of men consisted of a long horizontal pipe hanging over a gutter-like stream of water. This contraption was designed to carry away the excrement from the row of men perched along the pipe. On one occasion, likely to relieve the boredom of the journey, one of the soldiers thought it would be funny to light a piece of paper and let it float, burning, beneath the occupants of this primitive washroom. That incident caused considerable unwanted excitement for those involved, but temporarily provided many laughs for quite a few bored soldiers.

The North Atlantic was not kind to the Prairie men taking their first long ocean journey. There was stormy weather and rough seas for almost the entire trip and seasickness was a constant companion for most of the men. Bob was lucky to not be affected by seasickness. He survived the trip without incident.

Just seven days after sailing from Halifax, the Louis Pasteur berthed safely in the harbour at Greenock, Scotland, a major port and shipbuilding city of about 70,000 people situated 32 kilometres west of Glasgow.

Although he hadn't been sick on the ocean journey, Bob was glad to get his feet back on solid ground. He quickly found himself thinking, 'Thank God I didn't join the Navy!'

CHAPTER FIVE

Training in England

Although he had no recollection of the land of his birth, being in Scotland was slightly nostalgic for Bob Elliott. The city of Paisley, where Bob was born, was between Greenock and Glasgow and only 20 miles from where the Louis Pasteur had landed. His father's youngest brother, Archie, lived there with his wife Nan. Bob had hoped for a layover in Greenock so he could visit his uncle and aunt, but the Allied leaders had other plans.

The military gurus had exceeded themselves at troop transport efficiency this time and the soldiers were surprised to learn that a train was already waiting to take them to Aldershot Barracks in the south of England.

The speed at which they were transferred from one form of transport to another wasn't the only surprise for the newly arrived Canadians. They couldn't believe their eyes when they saw how small the trains were in England compared to the huge transcontinental trains they had ridden on at home.

"Where are we, Lilliput?" a young soldier asked as they approached a small train.

"Maybe if we look hard enough, we will find the name 'Dinky Toy' stamped on it somewhere," Bob mused as they gazed at the British train that they were about to board. Bob and his new friends thought this European train looked like it should be an amusement park ride and not a transport for soldiers, but the little train safely carried the young soldiers to Aldershot, 50 kilometres southwest of London.

'England really is a beautiful country,' Bob thought as the train passed through the countryside. 'So many trees and farms. Even in winter, this place has an old-world charm about it. So much history here, too.' Watching the countryside and the ancient castles along the way, the 730-kilometre trip to Aldershot Barracks seemed to pass quickly and Bob was at his destination before he knew it.

Aldershot was the main disembarking centre for incoming Allied troops from all over the world. The food there was good, too, which was a nice change from their usual bland and sometimes unrecognizable mess-hall fare. Shortly after arrival, the soldiers were given seven days leave complete with a free train pass for anywhere in Great Britain. This was Bob's opportunity to get acquainted with his Scottish heritage and he chose that option over the good food at Aldershot.

'I know where I'm going," thought Bob as he waited in line for his pass. 'Scotland! Bonnie Scotland!' He could hardly wait to meet all the relatives he'd heard so much about from his mom and dad.

With no time wasted, Bob was on his way back to Scotland, retracing the trip he had just made. This time, the train seemed to be going slower and taking much longer because of Bob's eagerness to get to his destination. He had the strange feeling that he was going home, even though he could not remember any of his time there before.

When he arrived at the home of his Uncle Archie and Auntie Nan, they welcomed him with open arms and showered him with affection befitting their own son. As a bonus, the home-cooked food they served was even better than the fare he had left behind at Aldershot.

"C'mon, Bob. Let's go down to the pub and meet some of my friends," Uncle Archie said after supper on Bob's first night at their home. "I'll show you how to get the most out of our rationed Scotch whiskey." Archie Elliott was a true, blue Scotsman and enjoyed a wee dram of whiskey now and then.

He was also very proud of his nephew Bob in his fine Canadian Army uniform.

"Give us a wee hauf and a dump for me and my son Bob," was his order to the bartender. Bob soon understood that Uncle Archie was asking for a shot of Scotch and a small beer. The war-time rationing only allowed one shot of Scotch per day per person, so after meeting Archie's friends and finishing their drinks in the first bar, Uncle Archie and Bob headed to another bar to order the same thing there. This pattern of going from bar to bar continued until they'd had their fill and were ready to go home, happy and content.

Bob felt honoured that his uncle would call him his son and they had many enjoyable nights together during Bob's leave. They visited the bars, sang along with the piano and sometimes sang at the top of their voices in the park on their way home as well.

After Bob's leave was over, instead of returning to Aldershot, he and his regiment were relocated to Hayward's Heath on the south coast of England, overlooking the English Channel. It was there that the kitbags they had packed several weeks earlier in Debert, Nova Scotia, were reunited with their owners. When Bob received his kitbag, he stared at it with a puzzled look on his face.

'What the heck?' he thought. Green shoots were poking out of the top of his bag. 'Oh, right! Bill's onions!' he realized as he remembered the vegetables he had packed for his brother. Sure enough, the much-wanted onions had grown right through Bob's clothes and out the top of his kitbag!

'Well, I guess there'll be no onions for John,' Bob thought with a laugh as he removed the sprouted vegetables from his clothing.

After settling into the new barracks, Bob went for a walk with some of the other soldiers to check out their new location. The soldiers came to a pub and decided that maybe a beer or two would be a good idea.

Once inside, Bob was surprised by his surroundings. 'We must be in the wrong place. There are women in here.'

The liquor licensing authorities in Canada did not allow women to frequent bars at that point, so the presence of women in bars in England came as somewhat of a shock to these Canadian boys. They retreated to the sidewalk, went around the corner and in another door. To their surprise, they found themselves back in the same pub, only now they were on the other side of the bar!

After finding out what a fun-loving and friendly group of people these English folks were, Bob and his Army friends spent many enjoyable evenings in these establishments. These were places where they could unwind and forget about the future day when they would be facing the enemy across the English Channel.

There was always a piano in the bar, and someone who could play the popular tunes of that era. Every tune played was accompanied by a chorus of young soldiers who were living as if there was no tomorrow. Sadly, for some of these soldiers, there weren't that many tomorrows left.

The residents of that part of England treated these young Canadian men as though they were close family. The soldiers were invited into their homes for meals, and efforts were made to ensure their stay at Hayward's Heath was enjoyable.

Meanwhile, the training on the base was rigorous, with long days of hard work and some struggles in communication. Their trainers were older British sergeants who had accents that Bob and his comrades had difficulty understanding. These sergeants knew what they were doing, however, and apart from a lot of 'What did he say?' questions being repeated down the line among the Canadian troops, the training sessions went well.

New 25-pound field guns were issued to the soldiers, and these were much improved over the guns from the First World War that the men had used in their training in Canada. The new 25-pounders were drawn behind gun tractors called quadrupeds.

These were big four-wheel-drive, flat-nosed vehicles that looked formidable and had real power and accuracy far beyond their predecessors.

England was too densely populated to operate these loud powerful weapons there, so the firing ranges were situated in a remote region of Wales. While training on one of their many visits to the firing range, a stray shell from an American gun operating at an adjacent range exploded close to Bob's gun, wounding three of his crew, one of them quite seriously. Some shrapnel hit the soldier in the mouth and destroyed his teeth and gums. The Americans were apologetic for that mishap and took the injured soldiers to their field hospital. There, the American surgeons performed 62 operations over a period of six months on the one soldier with the mouth injury before he was returned to his regiment.

During both World Wars, cigarettes were considered by soldiers to be as important as food. Almost every soldier smoked. It helped to calm their nerves and relieve the stresses of war. Bob was no different, and he later developed a passion for cigars. During his training time in England, Bob cursed the rationing and the German U-boats who sank some of the Canadian supply ships. Both these events led to cigarettes being an even scarcer commodity. The soldiers kept all their cigarette butts in a can and when desperation dictated, they broke the butts up and rolled these bits of tobacco into new cigarettes.

The Woodbine brand of cigarettes was the most available supply in England at the time, but Bob felt these were the worst cigarettes anyone could possibly imagine. They tasted nearly as bad as the ones rolled out of butts, he felt. Still, they were cigarettes and they were slightly better than nothing.

While in Europe, Bob kept his word to his mother and dutifully sent home half of his soldier's pay to be saved for when he returned after the war. This did not leave him much for pocket money so in his spare time from training, he worked for local farmers in the south of England. He helped with the harvest for 10 shillings a day, the equivalent of about $1.00 Canadian then. It wasn't much, but it helped to bridge the gap.

In the fall of 1942, Bob was stooking oats in a field overlooking the English Channel when he noticed a large number of ships at sea and wondered what was happening. He didn't have to wait long for an answer.

That evening, he and his comrades learned of the incredible number of casualties suffered by the 2nd Canadian Division during a failed attempt to invade Dieppe. Of the more than 6,000 Allied soldiers who participated in the raid (4,963 of them from the 2nd Canadian Division), more than 3,300 were killed, wounded or captured, including 907 Canadians who lost their lives. It seemed as though the Germans had known these troops were coming and were well prepared for the onslaught.

This was a terrible blow to all the soldiers training in England at the time. A great feeling of depression swept through the Canadian regiments. Saddened at the loss of so many of their fellow countrymen, the Canadians soon rallied in spirit with a strengthened determination to win that bloody war.

Every evening after training ceased, all the available tanks and field guns were placed to take aim along the beaches. A German invasion was never ruled out and being prepared for an attack was the order of the day. Some soldiers said an invasion was inevitable.

Bob's leadership abilities had not gone unnoticed by his superiors and in the spring of 1943, he and five other men were issued with an 'American Priest,' a nickname for a self-propelled Sherman tank fitted with a 105-millimetre (mm) gun. New training was required to learn how to operate this deadly beast. Bob loved the gun and quickly became highly skilled with it, landing 24 out of 25 direct hits on simulated targets. Bob earned the title of top gunner and was promoted to full bombardier, which included another small raise in pay.

The next task for the trainees was simulated beach landings, which meant a lot of time at sea in a landing craft. They loaded their tanks and all variety of military equipment onto these vessels, went out to sea and returned to land on the beaches. The soldiers in Bob's group all felt something big was afoot by the sheer vastness of this exercise and many rumours circulated among them. Nobody told them exactly what they were training for or where they would be going, though, so the rumours simply continued to circulate.

Many of the soldiers were still prone to seasickness and some periodically spent so long at sea that their regular rations were exhausted and hardtack and bully beef were needed to fill the gap. Hardtack was not among the soldiers' favourite foods. It resembled biscuits but was so hard that the soldiers joked they'd need jaws like a bulldog to bite into it. To eat it, Bob and his mates soaked the hardtack in water until it turned into a bland-tasting porridge. "God only knows what they're made of," Bob joked. "I guess that's why they're called hardtack. I suppose we could lay some out on the ground and drive the tank over them. That ought to soften them up."

The bully beef wasn't much better, in Bob's opinion. This was beef that had been specially canned for Army rations. Some soldiers suggested this was the beef they couldn't sell in butcher shops, or maybe it was dog food with a different label. In any case, these were sometimes the only rations available, so the men ate them.

Every time a simulated beach assault was performed, the equipment ended up covered in mud and saltwater. Bob's tank was no exception, so he and the crew had to continually clean and repaint it. It was impossible to get all the mud out of the tank's nooks and crannies and Bob thought that by the time they were done training, the paint on the tank would be half an inch thick with some mud mixed in as well.

By 1943, Bob's older brother Matt had joined the Royal Canadian Army. This brought the total number of Elliott brothers in the Canadian Forces who were training in England to four. John was a provost marshal or military policeman. Bill, the first of the four to arrive in England, was driving trucks. Bob was in the Armoured Division and now Matt was a driver for the military engineers. Bob would be 18 years old later that year. John would be 33, Bill was 29 and Matt was 19. The only Elliott brother still living in Canada was Charles. At age 11, he was still too young to enlist but, being an Elliott, he probably considered the idea.

While in training, leave was granted every three months and Bob looked forward to these breaks from his routine. He spent one of his early leave periods in London, where John was stationed. Although he had a great time with his oldest brother, Bob found that everything was too expensive in the big city and he couldn't enjoy his time there as much as he would have liked. So Bob decided that Paisley was where he would go every three months when his leave came due. Besides, he could work at the milk factory there and make a little extra spending money while on leave from the Army.

In mid-December, Bob started thinking about how wonderful it would be if all four Elliott brothers could get together at Uncle Archie and Auntie Nan's house for Christmas. He contacted his brothers to discover that he, Bill and Matt had coinciding leave at that time but John did not. Being a military policeman had some advantages, but leave at Christmas wasn't one of them. John had to be on duty at Christmas to ensure the correct behaviour of Canadian soldiers who might partake of too much Christmas cheer.

Christmas Day 1943 was on a Saturday, which meant that the Elliott boys could not only spend Christmas Day in Paisley, but New Years Eve as well! Bob, Matt and Bill all arrived together on the Sunday prior to Christmas. Two days later, a knock at the door announced the arrival of the fourth brother, John.

"How did you manage to get here?" Bob asked in surprise when his oldest brother walked in. While Bob was happy to see John, he was also concerned for his brother's welfare if he was

AWOL. "Did they change their mind about giving you leave for Christmas?"

"Well, no," John answered, "I had to deliver some prisoners to Glasgow and I thought that being this close to you guys, I'd just slip over here and have Christmas with you. I wouldn't miss this reunion, no matter what the consequences," John added.

This was exactly what Bob had wanted. All four of them at Uncle Archie's. What a great time this would be!

The Elliott brothers were all well-trained soldiers by now and knew the importance of keeping their uniforms in order. This meant daily pressing to maintain a sharp and well-disciplined appearance. "We should draw straws and instead of all of us having to iron the uniforms, the one who gets the short straw will get very good at pressing," Bob suggested.

Matt ended up with the short straw and was awarded the task of ironing all the uniforms during their stay in Paisley. Since it was an onerous task to press four uniforms instead of just one, Matt thought he would be creative with his pressing methods. His first solution was to lay the uniforms out on the floor and walk all over them. This idea wasn't successful and he inevitably had to borrow Auntie Nan's iron and ironing board. In no time, Matt mastered the uniform-pressing chore and the four young soldiers had sharp-looking uniforms to wear on every day of their vacation.

Although Matt lost out in the chore department, he made up for it in the party mode. He was a magnet for the ladies and there were always more women hanging on to him than he could handle at the parties they attended. One of these young women sang a song one night that stayed in Bob's memory for decades thereafter.

"If I could paint a memory that lives within my heart," it began. It was such a beautiful song to Bob. He had never heard it before and was never able to find a record of the song, but it created an indelible memory of the only time during the Second World War that he and his three brothers were all together.

There is a saying that time passes quickly when you're having fun, and that was certainly the case for the four Elliott brothers in December 1943. John, who was not supposed to be on leave, returned to London on the day after Christmas. His brothers heard later that John earned himself some extra duty as punishment for his indiscretion, but he told his superiors that the enjoyment he had in Paisley that Christmas was worth every moment of his allotted penalty.

Shortly after his other brothers returned to their posts, Bob's regiment was moved to Bournemouth on the south coast of England. A week or two later, they were moved again to an old mansion in Pool Harbour. There, they were literally living on top of one another with 12 soldiers crammed into each bedroom.

By April 1944, the number of Allied soldiers in the area had swelled considerably. Many of these new recruits were American. The upside of this was the availability of Lucky Strike cigarettes. The American soldiers didn't mind selling their cigarettes to their Canadian cousins and the Lucky Strikes were much better than Woodbines. The downside was that the pubs were so crowded that it was extremely difficult for a thirsty soldier to get a beer.

Bob learned later that there were well over three million troops in the area. No wonder it was so crowded. The escalation of troops gave rise to many rumours as to what was coming. The soldiers could feel that something big was afoot.

Their training became more intense, mostly concentrating on barges, landing craft, beachhead landings and physical fitness. Then, to achieve peak physical fitness, large groups of soldiers were whisked away for two weeks of commando training at Loch Find in Scotland. There, they ran from morning to night at double time, jumped off ships into freezing water, climbed rope ladders and pulled guns up mountains. By now, these young Canadians began to realize that their party time was over and the real work had begun.

Bob received his orders in early May 1944 that he was being transferred to the 19th Army Field Regiment, attached to the 3rd Division. His expertise with the 105-mm guns was badly needed there. This came as a blow to Bob. It was difficult to leave the crew that he had been with since the beginning, but it didn't take him long to fit in with his new crew and he soon realized that his fear of leaving his buddies was unfounded.

At about that time, Bob heard that his brother Bill had broken his leg playing football. He was considered unfit for military duty and sent home to Canada. While Bob was sympathetic toward his brother's injury, he wondered if perhaps this was a blessing in disguise for Bill, who would not have to face the impending battles with the chance of not surviving. Bill would also be able to marry his sweetheart, whom he had left behind in Canada, sooner than he had expected.

Later that month, Bob was enjoying leave in Paisley with his uncle and aunt when a telegraph came ordering him back to his regiment. This had never happened during his three years of training and the telegraph had an ominous undertone to it.

Saying goodbye to his much-loved uncle and aunt at the Glasgow train station was more difficult this time. With the uncertainty of when or whether they would see each other again, tears fell freely as they parted company.

Immediately upon Bob's return to the barracks, all soldiers except the drivers were transferred to a base along the beach at Southampton. This base resembled a prison camp in its lack of mobility for the soldiers. Provost marshals patrolled 24 hours a day to ensure that no one went anywhere. No orders were being given, so the soldiers knew that the training they had endured over the past three years was about to be put into action.

The waiting was intense. Not knowing where they were going or when they might leave was a strange feeling that preyed on their minds if they let it. To alleviate the agonizing wait, the soldiers played cards, exercised and just plain wasted time.

On June 4, 1944, all the troops were taken to the docks and reunited with their equipment. There were ships, boats, barges and landing craft as far as the eye could see. Southampton has one of the world's largest natural deep-water harbours. From what Bob could see, there were so many ships there on that day that he thought he might be able to walk from one side of the harbour to the other without getting a foot wet.

This was it. This was the day of reckoning. Bob felt apprehensive but relieved that this day had finally come. Then, due to bad weather in the English Channel, boarding was cancelled.

More waiting. More time to wonder what was ahead.

He didn't have to wait long, however. On the following evening of June 5, 1944, the huge flotilla of vessels of every shape and size imaginable finally left the safety of Southampton harbour, carrying the biggest invasion force ever assembled in the history of the world. More than 5,000 ships, 11,000 airplanes and 160,000 servicemen made up what was called Operation Overlord.

Later, it would simply be known as D-Day.

CHAPTER SIX

Hell on Earth

Never before had a military operation of this magnitude been undertaken. None of the soldiers involved knew what a history-making voyage they were taking part in until they were well out to sea.

The 3rd Canadian Division alone had 24 Landing Craft, Tank (LCTs) vessels for its four artillery regiments. The vessels carried a total of 96 Priest self-propelled field guns, one of which was for Bob's crew, 24 half-track armoured infantry vehicles and the 2,300 personnel required to man these weapons. The LCTs were slow in comparison to a warship, so they left the harbour at 10:00 a.m. to begin the 18-hour, 25-mile voyage into the unknown.

The officers in charge of each vessel had brought sealed orders on board from British Field Marshall Bernard Montgomery and Allied Supreme Commander U.S. General Dwight D. Eisenhower. These instructions were only to be opened after the operation was well underway.

Some time after nightfall, the top-secret orders were opened. "The eyes of the world are upon you. Operation Overlord has begun," the officer read. "We are going into battle. Our objective is to land in Normandy and liberate Europe from German occupation. The attack will begin at 0430 hours. Our regiment will land at 0700 hours and establish a beachhead from which we will press inland 10 miles to capture the city of Caen and the adjacent Carpiquet Airport. Now, try to get some sleep if you can. Good luck and God bless you all."

"Sleep?" Bob said to the soldier next to him. "How in the hell does a man sleep on a barge being tossed around like a cork? They could have picked a better night than this."

"Well, at least we know where we are going now," the other man replied. "I wonder if Jerry[5] knows, too."

The English Channel was as cruel that night as it had ever been. The flat-bottomed LCT was tossed about so badly by the ferocity of the waves, it performed every manoeuvre except to capsize. The only consolation was that the whole convoy was experiencing the same treatment.

There was one soldier, a small man of Chinese origin named Toi on Bob's LCT, who wished it would do just that – capsize and end this misery for all of them. Toi was so sick that he begged the others to throw him overboard. This was not a wish that any of the other soldiers wanted to comply with, so Toi had to suffer out the next few hours along with the rest of the men. He was not alone in his misery. A good portion of the soldiers were seasick on that journey.

God only knows what thoughts were running through the minds of this vast number of servicemen as they crossed the English Channel that night. Some wrote letters to their loved ones in the vain hope that they would be delivered, while others played poker to pass the time. These men were the spearhead of an invasion that would take months to complete and involve more than three million men. Some would later say that these men were the cannon fodder, taking the hit so that others could follow without incident.

On June 6, 1944, at 4:30 a.m., the huge guns of the Allied battle ships opened fire on the French coast of Normandy. The barrage of whistling shells passed right over the heads of the floating army that was ready and willing to hit the beaches.

Bob's LCT and all others like it approached the shore and opened fire from their tanks while still on board from 1,000 yards out. They continued firing until they were only 600 yards from the beach. This tactic was called 'softening up' the enemy.

[5] Jerry – slang for German soldiers

Between the huge explosive shells from the battleships and the bombardment the tanks delivered, the commanding officers expected a reasonably clear run for the infantry to land. The vessels carrying the tanks then went back out to sea while the infantry started inland.

The first Canadian infantry unit landed at 7:30 a.m. at Juno Beach and although Bob and his crew couldn't see what was happening, they knew by the massive number of shells and bombs exploding that all hell had broken loose for the men on the beach.

The Germans were well prepared for an attack, with concrete bunkers that protected their machine gun and anti-aircraft emplacements. They also had a formidable force set up in a big house near the beach, firing their guns from that location. The Queen's Own Rifles were assigned to attack and secure that house. They achieved this goal but lost more than 100 men within the 100 yards from the shore to that house. (The house was later restored as a memorial to the Queen's Own Rifles soldiers who lost their lives in that battle.)

Then the LCTs headed towards shore and it was Bob's turn to join the battle on land. No amount of training could have readied Bob or his comrades for what they were about to experience. Their LCT came to a halt. Down went the loading ramp and Bob's tank, the second in line, proceeded to drive off. Every previous landing they had accomplished during training had been onto dry land. This time, the vessel had stopped short and they were driving into six feet of water. Bob was at the controls and could feel the waves tugging at the huge Sherman tank. Now he understood the reason for the waterproofing and flotation devices they had installed before boarding the LCT in England.

Once on the beach, they came to a standstill. What they saw there was not something anyone should ever have to witness. Dead and wounded soldiers were strewn about the sand like broken, discarded dolls at a landfill. The combination of bodies and the burning and twisted wreckage of jeeps and infantry vehicles made progress impossible.

'I've got to be dreaming, and this is Hell!' Bob thought as he wondered what to do next. Before he could make a decision, the unimaginable happened. Their tank, loaded with extra fuel, ammunition and camouflage equipment, took a direct hit from a mortar bomb and burst into flames. Three of his crewmates were killed instantly.

Bob escaped being incinerated but had no recollection of how he managed to get out of the tank or even what he did after he escaped the inferno. All he remembered later was that he ran as hard as he could up that deadly beach, carrying his rifle. As soon as he reached the meagre cover of some bushes, Bob stopped to catch his breath and look back at where the burning tank stood.

'There's no way any living thing could survive in there,' he thought.

Six men had been assigned to that tank. They were supposed to split into two shifts to take turns operating the massive machine. The tank was to be their weapon as well as their home during battle. While a driver, sider and gunner were at the controls, the other three men were supposed to be hunkered down inside the tank's chamber, resting, eating rations or otherwise trying to keep their minds off the horrors around them.

It was later determined that the three members of Bob's crew were the only three members of the 19th Field Regiment to die that day on Juno Beach. Seventeen others in his regiment were wounded.

Bob felt sick from the loss of three of his close comrades. He didn't know what had happened to the remainder of his crew either, but this was not a good beginning to his first taste of conflict. Then he looked down at his left hand and saw that it was bleeding profusely. A piece of his left index finger had been blown off in the blast! There was no time to consider this injury, though. "I've got to make it to cover!" Bob told himself.

His thoughts were racing as he moved ahead and repeatedly fired his rifle in the direction of where he thought the Germans might be hiding.

Within a few minutes, he met a group of nine Canadian soldiers and fell in with them. Without a tank, Bob was just another infantryman, but with no equipment. The only thing he'd been able to save was his rifle. He had no pack with all his personal belongings in it, no emergency food and no ammunition except what was in the magazine of his trusty Lee Enfield 303 rifle.

Then he thought suddenly, 'Dammit! My cigarettes were in my pack!' Now he was really mad. It was bad enough losing his friends and his gear, but his cigarettes, too! 'Those damn Germans will pay dearly for that!'

The rest of that day was spent advancing little by little, shooting at the enemy and trying to avoid being hit by Allied bombers that were still pounding the Germans not too far ahead of the Allied ground troops.

Toward evening, one of the men in Bob's group found an abandoned German foxhole. This carefully constructed hole in the ground had an entrance just big enough for one man to get in or out. Once Bob and the other Canadian soldiers crawled down into the foxhole, they found a small room about eight feet by eight feet. It was lined with oilcloth and had a rug on the floor.

"Hey, look at this," Bob said, picking up a pair of silk stockings that were hanging on the wall. "I didn't know Jerry wore these things into battle." His comment earned a round of laughter. It was a little humour that was well appreciated at a time when humour was so far from reality.

Ten tired young soldiers spent their first night in France in that hiding place. Most of them got some sleep, but Bob did not. His finger was throbbing unbearably by then and the pain kept him awake. One of the other soldiers had bandaged the wound for him but he had no access to painkillers, so sleep was virtually impossible. With this injury on top of his accident in

Canada with the axe, Bob's left index finger was now shorter than the right index finger he'd shortened in the seeder in what seemed like a lifetime ago. It was just one more thing to think about on that horrible first night in battle.

The men decided they would take turns keeping watch. At one point during the night, the soldier on sentry duty started firing his rifle. "There was a German sneaking up on us with his pack on," he told the others as they quickly came out of their hiding place to check on the commotion. "I got him, though."

The rest of the night passed without incident. Emerging from their sanctuary at daybreak, the soldiers discovered the true identity of the 'German' that their sentry had shot.

An old cow with rounded horns lay dead nearby.

"I guess it could have been mistaken for a German soldier carrying a pack in the dark," Bob suggested with a smile.

Being a foot soldier wasn't how Bob wanted to fight the rest of the war, so he soon bid farewell to the infantrymen. "Thanks for the company, guys, but I'd better go and find the rest of my outfit," he told the men, and started on his way.

On June 8, just two days after their horrific landing on Juno Beach, Bob was reunited with Atchy and George, the remaining members of his original tank crew. Later that day, they were assigned to a new American Priest tank and placed under the command of Sergeant Craig, whom Bob knew from serving with him in the 13th Regiment. Sgt. Craig was one of the many soldiers who never used their first name.

The sergeant was accompanied by two more new crewmen named Walt Ward and Ernie Dawson. Shortly after introductions to each other, Atchy decided that Ernie looked like a duke, so he started calling him 'Duke.' The name stuck and from then on, Ernie Dawson was known to all his fellow soldiers as Duke.

The Allied Forces' intention of freeing the city of Caen within 24 hours of landing was not fulfilled. There would be a month of hard fighting and heavy losses before they achieved that goal. The Canadian armoured forces advanced just yards at a time, often firing their guns so much that the barrels were red hot. Then they had to drop back to allow the guns time to cool off before engaging in battle again.

Sgt. Craig was a mine expert and was away from the tank a good portion of the time, leaving Bob in charge. This was quite a responsibility for a 19 year old from the Canadian Prairies but Bob had already proven himself to be a fine soldier, always willing to carry out orders and able to lead when necessary. His undeniable ability in all areas of Army life had been tested on many occasions.

Bob had a tremendous respect for the Polish soldiers who fought alongside his crew on the way to Caen. He thought they had a special vendetta to fulfill in retaliation for the evil that Hitler had wrought against their country. It was while they were fighting beside each other that the troops were bombed by their own Allied aircraft.

Looking up at those big planes and seeing their bomb bays open right above him was not Bob's idea of fun. The planes were flying so low that Bob could read the numbers on the bombs while they were still in the bomb bays. The number of casualties from that mistaken bombing was unknown.

On another occasion, an American fighter bomber took out Bob's ammunition supply truck. Bob had watched that plane fly low overhead and then turn in a slow circle until it was about three miles away. Then, for some unknown reason, the pilot released a rocket that went right into the back of Bob's ammunition supply truck, completely destroying it.

"You dumb bastard!" Bob futilely yelled into the sky, "can't you so-and-so's see the big white stars painted on the roofs of our vehicles? German trucks have a cross on their roofs!"

Bob knew his insults couldn't be heard, but he hoped the pilot would somehow feel his anger as the plane disappeared into the sky. Luckily, the driver of the supply truck wasn't inside it at the time of the bombing.

For the most part, it seemed to Bob as though there was no communication between air and ground forces on this journey inland. Confusion was the order of the day. Bob often surmised that the only reason the Allies won in France was that the Germans were more confused than they were.

All this commotion and fighting was hard on Bob's nerves, and with no cigarettes to calm him, his fingernails became shorter than they had ever been. But he still considered himself luckier than most. Apart from some minor scrapes, bruises and a very sore left index finger, he was still in one piece.

About three weeks into their slow 10-mile struggle to Caen, there came a day that afforded a lull in the fighting. Bob heard that his old regiment, the 13th, was nearby, so he took a leave of absence from his post to go visit with a soldier who had been a good friend to him during his time in that unit. Jim Pickle had been a corporal when Bob knew him, but Jim had since been promoted to captain. They renewed their acquaintance with a long conversation, during which Jim talked Bob into finishing his high school education by correspondence.

"You can do your upgrade here," Jim said. "All you've got to do is ask your commanding officer to set it up and he'll get you all the necessary documents. Having your Grade 12 graduation will help you get a decent-paying job when you go home."

Bob took Jim's advice and later completed his Grade 12 while in the Army. He later would say that he didn't know whether he had become smarter or someone in authority had taken pity on him, but the lessons seemed to be a lot easier to him than he remembered them being when he was in school in Calgary.

During their visit that day, Jim told Bob about his own involvement with the Allied observation forces and that his work involved spotting enemy positions from a small plane. One afternoon awhile later, Bob witnessed a small plane being shot down over enemy territory. A few days after that, he learned that his good friend Jim Pickle had been in that plane.

Jim had meant a great deal to Bob, not just as a friend but as a mentor who taught him a lot about life. Bob never got used to the sense of loss at a time like that. It was another reason to hate the perpetrator of this senseless loss of good folks' lives. These losses became a catalyst that strengthened Bob's resolve to rid the world of that maniac Hitler.

Adolf Hitler and his whole damn evil regime!

While the Canadians were working on their first major objective of capturing Carpiquet Airport, Bob had his first encounter with the fanatical Hitler Youth. Bob couldn't believe his eyes as he watched those young men attack his tank with a hand-held machine gun! This was nothing short of suicidal, but these soldiers considered it an honour to die for the Fuhrer. It was horrifying for Bob to watch these teenagers run at his fully-armoured vehicle, but they were the enemy in this bloody war and his orders were to shoot them before they shot him.

The Canadians' first attempt to secure the airport failed due to overwhelming opposition from the well-positioned and dug-in Germans. It was clear that to continue the onslaught would be futile. Bob's division was ordered to withdraw. While no one wanted to quit, it was a necessary manoeuvre at this time.

While regrouping their forces and developing a new attack strategy, some radio signals were received from one of their own soldiers who had somehow been left behind enemy lines during the withdrawal. That soldier was Toi, the young Chinese man who had begged to be thrown overboard during the trip across the English Channel. The information that Toi later provided to the Allies about German positions was a major contributing factor in the success of the operation. On July 9, 1944, thanks to Toi's information, the Carpiquet Airport came under the control of the Allies.

The city of Caen was the Canadians' next objective. The Allied bombers had saturation-bombed Caen for so long that it was reduced to a large pile of rubble. Before Bob and his division could enter the city, the streets had to be cleared by bulldozers. There wasn't much exchange of gunfire. The heavy bombing had annihilated any resistance. This was a major victory for the Canadian Army. Now Bob's division crossed the river and headed south. Two more Canadian divisions, the 2nd and the 4th, and another Polish division joined their ranks at this point. The front of this army was five miles wide as they advanced on their next target, the city of Falaise.

While they were driving toward Falaise, the Germans dropped paratroopers on them. It didn't make sense to the Allies that the Germans would drop their soldiers right in the midst of an armoured division, but that's what they did. One of these men landed so close to Bob's tank that Bob thought the German was going to land right on top of them. The crewmen were surprised at how quickly this German infiltrator happily surrendered. Five 303 rifles pointed at him may have had a bearing on his decision as he handed over his weapons and was shuffled off to prison camp.

Duke recovered the parachute that their captive had left behind and began to busily cut it into strips.

"What are you going to do with that?" asked Bob as he watched his friend attack his project with the zeal of a man with a purpose.

Duke picked up one of the strips of cloth and wrapped it around his neck. "I'm making scarves for our guys to wear as a reminder of what happened here today," he said. "This is probably the easiest victory we will ever have in this war," Duke added, looking around at all the Germans literally dropping into their laps.

Duke wore his nylon scarf every day for the rest of the war and for a long time after it was over.

While on their way to Falaise, about two weeks after capturing Caen, Bob's regiment was pulled out of line and issued with new tanks. They were all assigned Sexton SP (self-propelled) field guns that were built to British specifications on a Canadian Ram chassis at the Montreal Locomotive Works. The Sexton SP fired 25-pound shells which were easier for the Allies to obtain during wartime. The machine had an open top, was driven from the right-hand position and had a crew of six.

Bob was pleased to work with this new machine. The constant heating and cooling of the 105-mm guns on the American Priest tank from firing so many thousands of rounds had caused them to become inaccurate. This new machine, which Bob and his crew referred to as 'the tank,' was so powerful that the upper structure of it had to be massively reinforced.

The Sexton SP weighed about 54,000 pounds, which translates to more than 25 tons, and carried 112 rounds of ammunition. Although some of the crew missed the 105-mm gun, Bob had trained on the 25-pounder in England and was quite comfortable with it.

The road to Falaise was long and bloody, with another mistaken Allied bombing of the Canadians and the Polish soldiers of General Maczeck's 1st Armoured Division. Three hundred men were killed and wounded this time by what is now known as 'friendly fire.' Bob would later say there was nothing friendly about it.

Despite strong opposition, the Allies were able to surround the German 7th Army at Falaise. There, the Allies started a relentless bombardment of shelling and aerial bombing that went on for several days. The Germans held on until virtually everything around them had been destroyed.

A day or two before the Allied victory at Falaise, Bob had parked the tank in a field nearby to take a break from the battle. He was sitting in the driver's seat with his head sticking out of the tank, talking to Walt Ward, one of his crewmates. Walt was leaning on the front of the tank chatting with Bob when a German 88 shell, obviously aimed at their tank, took the top off Walt's head, killing him instantly.

The gun loader, Duke, had witnessed this awful scene from the turret and instantly became so hysterical that Bob had a difficult time getting him to calm down and stop looking at the grisly remains of Walt's body. Getting Duke back into the tank was by no means an easy task, either.

It was another horrible tragedy in a horrible war. Bob said a quick prayer for Walt and drove his machine back to the battlefield. Bob knew that he had to get Duke away from the ghastly scene or he'd lose another man. For decades after that, though, Bob thought about his friend Walt and his tragic death.

The city of Falaise was considered captured by August 17, but the Germans didn't officially surrender until August 21, when 50,000 German soldiers relinquished their hold on the city.

Bob's crew drove into Falaise to witness one of the most sickening sights Bob had ever seen. As he looked out across that scene of devastation, he was horrified at the young ages of the enemy. There were dead German soldiers stacked four and five deep in places. Many of them were no more than 16 years old.

'Oh my God, these are some poor mother's children!' he thought as the tragedy of war enveloped him. Dead horses that the Germans had used to haul equipment were lying everywhere, too. With the temperature in the 30s, the smell of decaying bodies was so strong that even the crews of the airplanes passing overhead at 500 feet had a hard time trying not to vomit. The horrors of war were starting to take their toll on Bob. How much more of this senseless killing would he have to endure?

While the battle for Falaise raged, General George Patton had been leading the U.S. Army into Paris. On August 25, the Germans in Paris surrendered and France was freed from Hitler's iron grip. The Allies then turned their attention to freeing Belgium and the Netherlands.

Bob's tank, along with all the rest of their Army's field equipment, was loaded onto tank trailers for the journey across Belgium. By the time they reached the border, the British had ousted the Germans from most of Belgium. Bob and his crew were ordered to head directly to Antwerp to free that all-important port and secure it for the landing of Allied reinforcements.

A replacement soldier for Walt Ward joined Bob's crew as they were crossing into Belgium. He introduced himself as Conroy and never said if that was his first name or last. No one asked, so he was always known to the crew as Conroy.

The tank hauler dropped off Bob and his crew about halfway across Belgium. In later years, Bob would say that they lost their way while passing through the city of Ghent. In actuality, they 'got lost' outside a pub where they could ask for directions as well as relax for a few minutes. Enjoying a few beers was a huge treat after all the horrors they had experienced.

The Belgian people were celebrating their new freedom and they enjoyed having this Canadian tank crew as their guests. Bob and his men were treated to many free drinks.

By the time the Canadians reached Antwerp, the city and its port had been secured by the British but the Scheldt estuary leading to this important location from the North Sea was still under German control. Both sides of that long narrow waterway were heavily fortified with German gun emplacements. Allied shipping vessels had to pass through the estuary to unload precious cargo at Antwerp, so the Canadians were given the daunting task of clearing out the Germans to allow safe shipment of Allied supplies. Bob would later call the Battle of the Scheldt the worst of his experiences during his time in action.

The first time they tried to enter the Netherlands to clear out the Germans, they failed. They walked into a heavily fortified German position, swiftly withdrew and regrouped. They did more reconnaissance and then moved into the Netherlands again not far from the port city of Bergen op Zoom. There, they enjoyed two days of rest before engaging the enemy along the Scheldt.

The Germans blew holes in the dykes along the estuary, causing extensive flooding of the lowlands. This action had the desired effect of hampering the advance of the Canadians in their bid to free the waterway to Antwerp. The only roads left were along the tops of the dykes, which exposed the Allies as easy targets for the dreaded German 88 field guns. These guns were so well dug in that their only visible part was about two feet of barrel, which was a difficult target to hit. One 88 gun held up the entire Canadian Army for several days. An air attack from an Allied mosquito squadron finally took care of the bothersome guns.

Clearing the waterway was a slow and painful battle for the infantrymen. Soldiers were often up to their waists in water for days at a time. The Canadians ran out of ammunition and food, having been cut off from their supply line for several days. Bob's crew could not use their weapon and the soldiers were forced to fight the Germans with the only weapon they had, their bayonets. Losses were high and help from the British Forces was delayed due to Field Marshall Bernard Montgomery's botched attack at Arnhem. The Brits did rescue the Canadians eventually, but that battle left an indelible mark on the memories of the surviving soldiers.

After Scheldt, the last stronghold to be overcome was Walcheren Island, at the mouth of the Scheldt estuary. There, after crossing the waterway to the island on a temporary pontoon bridge, most of Bob's regiment was cut off by a German counterattack. For three days, they had no ammunition, no food or water, and bayonets as their only weapons. The only thing they could do to survive in that mudhole was to hope for a miracle. The British arrived just in time to help bring this deadly battle to a successful conclusion and on November 7, 1944, Walcheren Island was finally secured.

The graveyards at Bergen op Zoom later became a lasting testament to the heavy price paid by Canadians for the securing of the Scheldt estuary. Thousands of Canadian soldiers were killed in that battle. It was fitting that the first Allied supply ship to berth at Antwerp was Canadian.

After the battle, Bob and his crew returned to Bergen op Zoom for another few days rest while waiting for their next assignment. "You will drive your tanks northeast to the town of Alphen on the Maas River, where you will join up with the Fort Garry Horse Regiment to take up a holding pattern for the winter," they were told.

The trip to this new location north of Hertogenbosch in the Netherlands was relatively uneventful except for the cheering their columns of troops and armoured divisions received from the Dutch people who lined the roadsides to welcome them. Bob and his fellow Canadians were overcome by the poorly dressed and emaciated condition of these people. Almost five years of German occupation had taken a terrible toll on their way of life. Still, they seemed to have never lost hope.

ROBERT ELLIOT

JOHN ELLIOT

WILLIAM ELLIOT

MATTHEW ELLIOT

Above: Aldershot Barracks, England.
Photo - www.archhistory.co.uk

Left: The four Elliott brothers during the Second World War. John was born in 1910, Bill in 1914, Matt in 1924 and Bob in 1925. Charles was too young to enlist, born in 1932.
Photos – courtesy of Bill Elliott

Above: Convoy on its way to Juno Beach. The LCTs were slower and larger than these vessels and had started out many hours earlier. Photo – www.armouredacorn.com

Right: Queen's Own Rifles house, German stronghold on Juno Beach.
Photo: www.normandy1944.info

Below left: American Priest Sherman tank.
Photo – wwww.armorama.com

Below right: Sexton SP – The self-propelled field gun which Bob and his crew called their 'tank.'
Photo – wwww.armouredacorn.com

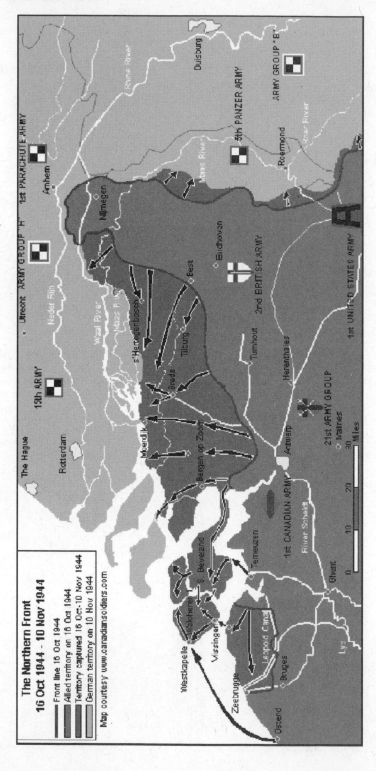

The Northern Front
16 Oct 1944 - 10 Nov 1944

Front line 16 Oct 1944
Allied territory on 16 Oct 1944
Territory captured 16 Oct-10 Nov 1944
German territory on 10 Nov 1944

Map courtesy www.canadiansoldiers.com

CHAPTER SEVEN

Escape!

September 25, 1944 was a warm sunny day in Rossum, which was a brief respite from all the rain the town had received for most of that month. At about 3:00 p.m., Willem was talking to one his Dutch Resistance contacts on the street outside the Cretiers' home. The two men were standing beside their bicycles, deep in conversation.

"Word has come from our sources that the SS suspect you of working with the Resistance," the contact quietly told Willem. "We think it is time for you and your family to make your escape. The Allies are only six kilometres from here at the Maas River near Alphen and if you…"

Just then, a group of noisy SS storm troopers on bicycles came around a corner just two blocks away. After what his friend had just said to him, Willem immediately panicked.

'This is it! This is the arresting party and they're coming for me!' he thought.

So Willem jumped on his bicycle and rode off as fast as he could.

On seeing Willem's reaction, Willem's friend bolted as well.

Willem did not know that this was not an arresting party at all, but just a group of SS men with a little too much alcohol under their belts. However, as soon as the Germans saw the Dutch men bolt away from them, they immediately gave chase.

"Halt!" one of the SS men yelled. The Germans believed that anyone running away from them must automatically be guilty of something, and these two obviously had no intentions of stopping.

The Germans started shooting. The chase intensified with a hail of bullets being fired.

Geert's heart sank when she looked out her window and saw Willem and his friend being chased by the Germans. Willem had narrowly escaped execution by firing squad only a few days earlier, and now this!

"What's happening?" Sussie asked fearfully when she heard the commotion.

Geert grabbed her children and held them close.

"Don't worry. Everything will be alright," Geert said quietly. Then after an awkward silence, she added, "I don't know if we will see Dad again, though."

Sussie wondered how her mother could remain so calm when something so awful was obviously happening to her father. Then Sussie looked up and saw the tears in her mother's eyes and knew that her mother was very close to the end of her endurance.

Sussie loved her father dearly and the thought of losing him brought tears to her own eyes. She couldn't imagine life without her dad.

Geert continued to hug her children together, trying to comfort them in their anguish. Outside in the streets, the chase continued.

One of the SS members held a young local boy against the side of a building and screamed at him, "Which way did he go?" The muzzle of the German's pistol was pressed hard against the boy's head. "You must have seen him. He went right by here! Tell me where he went or I will shoot you right now!"

The terrified young man pointed in the direction he had last seen Willem. "He... he went that way," stammered the boy. "But I...I...I don't know where he is now."

An older relative of the boy who was watching this altercation collapsed at the sight of his nephew's plight.

Neighbours feared the old man had died from fright but found later that he had only fainted.

Willem eluded capture by using his knowledge of the alleys and lanes of Rossum. He ditched his bicycle in a woodshed at the back of a bakery, threw some firewood over the bike and ran as fast as he could to the house of his friend, Minister de Jong.

"They are after me!" Willem gasped as he rushed into the de Jongs' home. "Don't tell them I am here!"

Mrs. de Jong and her two-year-old son Keesje were home at the time. The minister was out visiting members of the church. Willem raced up the stairs, climbed out the window onto the roof and hid in the wide eavestrough surrounding the house.

The group of Germans arrived at the de Jong home. "You will come out now!" their leader screamed, suspecting Willem was inside. "Come out now or we will blow up your house!"

Without waiting for a response, they hurled a grenade through the window. It exploded in the kitchen, blowing off cabinet doors and shattering dishes. Keesje and his mother had been in another room and safe from the explosion, but the young boy became hysterical and started screaming.

A German officer joined the SS group at that point and yelled at his comrades, "Stop! Stop right now! Who are you looking for here?"

"We don't know," a spokesman for the SS replied. "We were just coming through town and two men ran from us, so we gave chase. We think one of them is hiding in this house."

As the men were speaking outside, Mrs. de Jong came down the steps with her sobbing child in her arms. "What do you think you are doing?" she asked sternly. "You have terrified my son and destroyed my kitchen. You have no reason to do these awful things! We are innocent people and my husband is a minister."

"We have reason to believe there is a man in your house wanted for questioning," the officer said. "I'm sorry for the actions of my men but I do need to search your home."

They proceeded to search the house thoroughly but failed to find Willem. His hiding place had served him well.

"I saw a man running toward the dyke just before you came," Mrs. de Jong offered. "Maybe he is the one you are looking for."

This explanation seemed to satisfy the Germans and they left to continue their search elsewhere.

As Willem lay in the safety of the gutter, many thoughts ran through his mind. He thought the SS men were after him and he formulated his plans to escape.

'What do I do now? Where will I go? If I go home, they will catch me for sure. I could go stay with Geert's Aunt Tanteke in Heerewaarden. That's only about three kilometres from here and closer to the Allies. If I can just get over that bridge by the lock, I know I could get there. Then I could get a message to Geert.'

The bridge in question had guards posted who questioned every civilian who approached before deciding whether to allow them to cross or not. Getting through that checkpoint would not be easy, but if anyone could convince the guard of his innocence, Willem was sure that he could.

A few minutes after the Germans left the de Jong house, Willem came down from his hiding place, thanked Mrs. de Jong and apologized for the mess he had created. Then he headed out into the town, using the alleys to remain hidden.

Back at the Cretier home, 12-year-old Kees could not control his desire to know what had happened to his father. "Mom, I'm going to go out and look for Dad. I have to know if he is alright,"Kees said.

"Okay," Geert agreed, knowing the danger her son would be in. "I think we all need to know that."

Kees left their home as nonchalantly as he could. He didn't want to arouse suspicion by hurrying or looking nervous. He wanted to appear to be a young boy who was only going for an afternoon stroll.

"I think they shot Willem Cretier," Kees overheard one of the neighbours say as he walked by, but Kees wasn't sure if the neighbour had said, "shot Willem Cretier," or "shot at Willem Cretier." Either way, this talk was of no comfort to Kees.

Whether it was by good luck or family intuition, Kees sauntered into the very alley where Willem was hiding.

"Kees, Kees! Over here!" Willem called softly.

Hearing his father's loud whisper calling his name was the best thing Kees had heard since the chase began a half hour earlier. As Kees drew near to his father's hiding place, Willem held a finger up to his lips indicating a need for caution. Kees had never seen his father look as scared as he did now.

"Could you do me a big favour?" Willem asked nervously.

"Anything. Anything at all," Kees said, grateful that his father was still alive.

Willem continued, "I left my bike under a pile of wood in the bakery woodshed at the other end of this alley. Could you go and get it for me? I even locked it so you'd better take the key."

"Sure," Kees answered. "Anything you need," and off he went with the key in hand.

Finding the woodshed was no problem for Kees, but Willem's bike was buried under a large pile of firewood. In his haste to hide this damning evidence, Willem had caused an avalanche of wood to fall on top of his bike. Kees worked hard to remove the debris and free his father's much-needed transportation. When he finally wrenched it free from the shed, the bike landed on its side. Willem's saddlebag flew open and out fell a loaded handgun and a Dutch/English dictionary. Kees quickly picked up the gun and the book and put them back in the saddlebag.

His emotions were mixed as he rode the bike back to where his father was hidden. He was so proud of his father for his Resistance involvement but at the same time, so afraid for his father's safety.

Willem was happy to have his bike back and had one more request of his son. "Now, could you go to the bridge by the lock, see how many guards are there and report back to me?"

Again, Kees knew he would have to assume an air of indifference as he ambled down to the vicinity of the bridge, gathered the information and walked slowly back to Willem. It was so hard for him to appear unhurried when every second wasted potentially closed the window of opportunity for his father's escape.

"The bridge appears to still be open and there is only one guard," Kees reported to his father.

Willem was thrilled to hear this news. "That's great," he said. "I am going to try to make it to Aunt Tanteke's in Heerewaarden. If I get there, you will hear from me soon." He gave his son a quick hug, mounted the bike and rode down to the bridge.

Kees watched his father's departure with an overwhelming feeling of anxiety. "Dear God, if you ever answer any of my prayers, answer this one," Kees prayed as he watched Willem ride away. "Watch over my father and keep him safe. Amen."

Kees strained his eyes to watch while Willem stopped to talk with the guard for what seemed like a long time. Then Willem mounted his bicycle and rode off toward Heerewaarden.

Kees waited another five minutes to be sure his father was out of danger and, hearing no gunfire, he assumed that his father's escape had been a success.

Walking back to their house from the bridge area took Kees about 15 minutes. Even though Kees wanted to run, he knew he had to walk slowly. He could not draw attention by hurrying.

"I think Dad got away," Kees whispered in his mother's ear as soon as he got inside.

"Oh," Geert replied. "Good," as she gave a sigh of relief. Then she wondered to herself, 'What happens now?' She didn't have to wait long for an answer.

Shortly after 4:00 p.m., Pastor Daniels arrived at their door with a stern look of concern on his face.

"Willem is safe," he said quietly as Geert let him in. "He made it to your aunt's place in Heerewaarden but you have to leave, too. The Gestapo has identified him as the man they chased earlier today and they have placed him on their Wanted List. They are on the way now to arrest you and the children. By arresting you, they hope to force Willem to give himself up, so there isn't much time."

The urgency in his voice convinced Geert she had no alternative but to take her children and go to her husband. To stay in their home would mean death for all of them.

"Put on the warmest clothes you have and get the bikes ready," Geert told Sussie, Kees and Gerard as soon as the minister left their house. "Dad is safe in Heerewaarden and we must go to him now. The Germans are coming for us."

The children wasted no time doing what their mother asked. They dressed quickly and left their home, locking the door behind them. They had only two bicycles now. Geert rode one with Gerard riding on the carrier and Kees rode the other with Sussie riding on his carrier. Atoz the dog was the only thing they took with them other than the clothes they were wearing.

Leaving the house they grew up in was difficult for all of them. There were so many good memories there. They could only hope that everything would still be there when they returned after the war was over.

"Halt!" the German soldier on duty challenged as Geert and her family approached the bridge over the canal.

Anxiety and fear had been constant companions of the Cretiers for a long time but, with practice, they had learned how to conceal their emotions from the Germans. They stopped their bicycles and dismounted by the sentry.

"Where are you going?" he asked.

"We need to go see my mother in Heerewaarden," Geert said, pointing. "She is very ill and we need to go and take care of her," she lied.

The sentry studied them for a moment. "Why do you have your children and this dog with you?" he asked.

Geert, always able to create plausible explanations regardless of the situation, replied, "I can't leave them home alone where there's nobody to take care of them. Also, this dog is still young and would make a big mess if left alone."

The sentry accepted Geert's explanation and let them pass.

"Just walk normally," Geert whispered to the children when they were far enough away that the guard could not hear her. "We don't want to appear to be in a hurry and attract attention."

As soon as they mounted their bikes, they heard the telephone at the guardhouse on the bridge ringing.

They had made it.

The three-kilometre bicycle ride from the bridge to Geert's aunt's house was without incident. It was wonderful to be reunited with Willem, but now they were fugitives in a different town that was under German rule. They had to be very careful.

A message from the Resistance came to them the next morning. All the residents of Rossum were being evacuated and sent north, away from the lines of battle. Only a few essential people would remain. The bridge back to Rossum would be open for only one hour beginning at 10:00 a.m.

"We had better go back to our house and get some of our things while we have the chance," Geert suggested to Willem.

"That's a good idea," Willem replied. "But I can't go. They would recognize me for sure."

"I'll go," Kees offered. "They don't know me and I'm sure I could get through."

"I'll go with you," Geert said, proud of her brave son. "Even if I have to wait at the bridge, I can help carry our things from there." So Geert and Kees went on the bicycles to make the most of their one-hour period of grace.

"When you get to our house, Kees, I want you to find as many clothes as you can for all of us. I think that's all we'll need," Geert instructed her older son as they rode toward the bridge they had crossed the previous afternoon.

Luck was with them again. The same guard who let them pass the day before was on duty, and he did not know that this was the family the Gestapo had been seeking. "Where are you going this time?" the guard asked when they stopped beside him. "And where are your other children?"

"My other two are at my mother's," Geert answered. "We just want to get some things we need from home. My son can go and get them and I'll wait here if that's alright."

The guard studied them for a moment. "I don't suppose a young boy can do any harm, so off you go. But be sure to be back within the hour or you will be denied crossing."

Geert waited patiently and a little anxiously for her son's return. Kees was back within the allotted time with many of their much-needed belongings. Geert stowed some of their clothes onto her bike and they set off side by side back to Heerewaarden. Every few minutes, Geert looked across with admiration at her brave young son, thankful for a successful conclusion to their quest.

The family shared a few well-needed laughs when they saw some of the items that Kees had rescued from their home in Rossum. In the stack of clothing was a particularly large number of baby bibs. "Why did you bring all these bibs?" Geert asked as they were unpacking the clothes.

"I was in a hurry," Kees replied. "I just grabbed anything I could see and I didn't even look at what they were."

"Well, I don't think we'll be in need of those," Geert said with a chuckle. She hugged her son once again in appreciation of his courage.

Heerewaarden was between the Waal and the Maas rivers, between the opposing armies. Although the Germans thought they had total control of Heerewaarden, small groups of Canadian soldiers were infiltrating the town during the day to gather information on German positions. At night, German soldiers patrolled the streets. Willem was concerned about his family's precarious position there and the danger that they had caused to Geert's aunt, especially when he realized that the nighttime patrols were searching for them!

About 10 days after their initial escape from Rossum, the Cretiers had their first frightening experience at Geert's aunt's house.

"You all have to get down under the floor tonight. The Germans are nearby and I think they are looking for you," Aunt Tanteke said with urgency as she opened the hidden hatch to her crawl space.

Quickly, the Cretier family and their dog Atoz slipped down the hatch and crawled over to hide behind the piers that held up the floor. A loud banging at the front door came soon after they were hidden. Aunt Tanteke cautiously opened the door.

"Have you seen a family with three children and a dog?" a German soldier asked her.

"No," Geert's aunt replied. "I don't go anywhere these days, so I haven't seen anybody."

The hidden fugitives lay still, barely able to breath for fear that the soldiers would hear them. Atoz lay still and quiet, too, as if he knew exactly what to do. This time, the soldiers left without searching the house but they came back again two nights later.

"Quick! Get down under the floor again. The Germans are back!" Aunt Tanteke instructed the Cretiers. Willem and his family snuck down into the crawl space again and tried to be quiet.

"We have reason to believe that the family we seek is here," said the same soldier who had visited earlier. "We are going to search your home," he continued as he and his patrol forced their way inside.

Fear coursed through the veins of the family hiding below the floor as they listened to the clomping of boots above them and the sound of the soldiers ransacking their aunt's house.

"Dear God, let no one sneeze or cough right now," Willem silently prayed. They had survived more than four years of Nazi rule. To be captured now when freedom was so close would be tragic.

The search above them came to an end and the Germans left without finding anything. After Willem was sure the Germans had gone, he whispered to Geert. "Tomorrow, we will make our escape. This is too dangerous for us and for Aunt Tanteke. It's only a matter of time before they find us." They decided that, first thing in the morning, they would make a run for the Maas River to the safety of the Allied lines.

* * * * *

Dawn was breaking when the Cretiers left Geert's aunt's house. They took only the clothes they were wearing. No bicycles. Nothing heavy.

Trees, shrubs and hedges gave them cover for the first kilometre of their journey. The final two-kilometre stretch was open road that ran close and parallel to the Maas River as it turned south and away from the Waal River. Their destination was a dyke that protected the north side of the Maas as the river turned east again. The Canadian Army had set up a battle line there, on the river side of the dyke.

On the north side of the Waal River in the small town of Varik, the Germans had set up an observation and machine gun platform in the steeple of the church. The open road that Willem and his family had to travel to safety was clearly visible from this lofty German viewing point.

Willem gathered his family together when they reached the end of the protected part of their journey. He had gone over this scene in his mind many times, but he had not found any other way to avoid the next part of his dangerous plan.

They had to run to safety.

"Now, when you start to run, run as fast as you can!" he told the children. "You must weave, duck, slow down and speed up so as not to make yourself an easy target. Don't hold hands and don't run close to each other. The further apart we are, the harder it will be for them to hit us."

Willem pointed to the dyke where the safety of the Allied Forces was waiting. "Now, when I say 'GO!' you run for that dyke. Don't look back. Just run for your life! The Allies are on the other side of that dyke."

Ten-year-old Sussie was terrified. Her legs felt like they were stuffed with cotton balls. The dyke looked so far away.

"Go!" Willem said loudly.

The moment that the Cretiers broke cover and started to run, the Germans began shooting at them. Kees took the lead. He was a fast runner and was soon well out in front. Atoz was up there with him, running like crazy, too.

To every member of the Cretier family, those two kilometres seemed like the longest journey in the world. With bullets flying all around them like scores of angry bees, the brave family ran like they had never run before, ducking and weaving as Willem had told them to do. The safety of that 10-metre dyke seemed so far away and every second seemed like an eternity. Geert was tiring quickly and gasping for air. Running the gauntlet was hardly her forte.

"Keep going!" Willem called to Geert. "You've got to keep going! You can do it!"

From the other side of the dyke, Canadian soldiers from the Fort Garry Horse Regiment were watching the Cretiers' progress through binoculars.

"We got us a family escaping from the Germans," their officer said. "Give them some covering fire and get ready to bring them over the dyke!"

The Canadians started shooting at the Germans' position.

Kees was the first to climb the dyke. "Get down and crawl across the top!" the Canadians yelled at him. Kees didn't understand English so he didn't understand what they said to him, but he could tell by their gestures what they meant. Sussie and her father were next, followed closely by Gerard.

"When you get on top of the dyke, get down and crawl across as fast as you can!" Kees was yelling to them in Dutch. Geert was so tired when she reached the top of the dyke that she couldn't get down and crawl. Allied soldiers were yelling at her to get down but they quickly realized that she was too exhausted and one of the Canadians went to her rescue and carried her to safety.

"We made it!" Willem said, ecstatic. It was unbelievable!

"We all made it!" he repeated. "Even Atoz! Is everyone alright?"

They checked each other for possible wounds and found nothing. They had all escaped without injury! This was truly a miracle!

The Cretiers hugged each other with tears in their eyes, so thankful that none of them had been shot. The Canadians were cheering and offered the Cretiers tea, chocolate and fruitcake. What a treat those items were for a war-torn family. It had been a long time since they had eaten anything that tasted that good.

'Wow, this tea is strong,' Sussie thought as she took a drink. 'More sugar, that's what it needs. Much more sugar. That chocolate tastes soooo good!' She couldn't remember the last time she had eaten chocolate.

Conversation with the Canadian soldiers was a very difficult process. Willem was the only one who understood some English and his ability to communicate with the soldiers was limited. Sussie resolved to learn English so she could talk to these brave men. Meanwhile, she and her brothers just sat quietly and listened.

Now, what to do with a family of five and their dog? This was the new dilemma for the Allied soldiers. They knew the family couldn't stay at the front line, but news of the Cretiers' escape preceded them and a member of the Dutch Resistance soon arrived to talk to the Cretiers.

"We have made arrangements with a farmer and his wife near Alphen for a room for you and your family to stay in," the

Dutch Resistance member told Willem. "I will take you there now."

Willem shook hands with the Canadian soldiers and thanked them for the tea, cake and chocolate. Gathering up his family, he followed his Resistance comrade to the place the Cretiers would call home for the remainder of the war.

Willem and Geert held hands as they walked away from the Allies. They silently thanked God for delivering them all safely out of the hands of the Nazis.

CHAPTER EIGHT

Bob meets the Cretiers

It had been one month since the Cretiers' terrifying escape. They were living in one room, sharing the tiny kitchen of an old farmhouse with a leaky roof. The house had no indoor plumbing and the outhouse was built in an old nearby barn. Willem and Geert had an old bed to sleep on but the children had to share a mattress on the floor. Every time it rained, water leaked through the roof and onto their makeshift bed. When this happened, Geert covered the children with old waterproof capes to keep their bedding dry.

'This is still better than living under German rule,' thought Sussie as she and her brothers struggled to fall sleep while listening to the drops of water falling on their covers.

The old farmer who owned the house was a tall, thin man not known for his sense of humour. He and his wife had no offspring and they weren't used to having spirited children around their home. Gerard in particular was often in trouble.

"Who put water in my shoes?" the farmer yelled one morning. "I'll give them a lickin' they won't forget!"

Fortunately, Geert had a natural talent for calming those whose anger was getting the better of them. "Please don't be too hard on the children," she said to the farmer quietly. "They just do things without thinking sometimes."

Geert knew that the mischievous Gerard was the most likely one to have pulled this prank, and she scolded him later for this misdemeanour. Gerard never repeated the trick.

The farmer's wife was a very proper lady who always dressed as though she was going to the opera. Sussie didn't appreciate the wife's cooking skills much, but Sussie believed that her own mother was the best cook in the world, so the farmer's wife didn't stand much of a chance in that category. The wife was an excellent pianist, however, and the tunes she played were etched in Sussie's memory for many years.

To Sussie, the town of Alphen wasn't as tidy as Rossum and she missed her hometown's neat streets and pretty flowers. Although the condition of Alphen was likely due to four and a half years of German occupation, Sussie only saw it as being messy.

Then there were the rats.

The outhouse barn was infested with these rodents and Sussie hated when she had to go out to the building at night. It was so dark and spooky and full of strange noises that her nighttime visits there were terrifying. To make matters worse, her brothers thought it was funny to take advantage of her fears. They made terrible noises, hid in the dark and jumped out at her for fun. Sussie yearned for the day when they could all go back to Rossum and live a normal life again.

* * * * *

The morning of November 12, 1944, began much the same as any other day at that time in Alphen's history. For the Cretiers, it involved trying to find enough food to feed their family, and they were preparing to do this again when they heard a distant rumble that grew slowly louder.

"What is that strange noise? Geert asked. "I have never heard anything like that before."

"I don't know," Willem replied. "It's too constant for thunder, and it's not bombers."

Then there was loud shouting coming from the street.

"Come and see what's happening!" someone yelled. "This is incredible!"

The Cretiers quickly went outside and saw that the streets were lined with hundreds of people waving and welcoming an endless column of tanks, trucks and soldiers. Salvation had finally arrived!

Although Canadian soldiers from the Fort Garry Horse Regiment were already in Alphen, the people of the town now knew by the sheer size of this approaching army that their time of oppression was truly over and that it wouldn't be long until the war was just a memory.

* * * * *

Bob Elliot was at the controls of his Sexton SP as the 19th Field Regiment and the 55th Infantry Battalion of the Canadian Army moved into Alphen that day. Bob was worried he might run over the local people as they swarmed around the monster machine he was driving and climbed onto the tank to hug their liberators. He had to stop the machine on many occasions to avoid crushing some of the people who welcomed the Canadian soldiers so warmly.

As Bob looked at the crowd of happy faces, he knew that all the pain and suffering he had endured since landing in Normandy had been worth every moment. Tears came to his eyes as he saw the joy and gratitude on the faces of these people who had endured five years of oppression. Being a member of the Army that had freed them was a humbling experience. He knew he would never forget these moments.

Bob Elliott had never thought of himself as a hero. He was just a soldier doing his job, but this happy crowd certainly thought of him and all the other Canadian soldiers as heroes. The Dutch people had been saved and the Canadians had saved them!

The tanks and infantrymen were finally able to make their way to the east end of Alphen, where they created a long line of tanks and artillery that was protected from the prying eyes of the Germans by a 30-foot-high dyke. Bob and his crew began to think about servicing their weary tank with all the repairs and maintenance it so badly needed. It had been a long hard trail for the machine and its crew. But first, they were looking forward to a decent meal and a good night's sleep.

During battle, the soldiers relied on the rations they had in their possession. When they were stationery, a cook wagon travelled down the line and the soldiers approached it with their mess cans and cups in hand to be served their meal. Arriving in Alphen seemed like a pleasant respite compared to their previous few months of battle.

The next morning, while compiling a list of all the repairs the tank needed, Bob's crew was approached by a small Dutch girl who appeared much younger than her 10 years. Her clothes were worn to an almost threadbare condition with her elbows showing through the sleeves of her coat. Her well-kept blonde hair was tied up in neat pigtails, however, and indicated a preservation of her self-respect in contrast to the condition of her clothes. She also had a brightness in her eyes that seemed to say, 'I know in my heart that everything is going to be alright.'

"Could you please give me some cigarettes for my papa?" she asked the soldiers with her thick Dutch accent and big pleading brown eyes. The hearts of these battle-hardened soldiers quickly went out to her. She could have been their little sister. Bob himself was only nine years older than her, a couple years less than the age difference between Bob and his older brother Bill.

"Sure," Bob said as he and his men responded to her request. "Here, have some chocolate and chewing gum, too."

Sussie carefully placed the cigarettes in an old battered tobacco tin she carried with her. Then she put the chocolate and gum that she intended to share with her brothers into her pocket. She politely thanked the soldiers as best she could in English and went on her way.

"Boy, these people have had a rough time under the Germans," Bob observed as he watched the young girl continue down the line of tanks and field guns, asking other soldiers for whatever they would give her. "I wish there was more that we could do for them."

The girl returned later that day with a thin man of average height, whom Bob thought might be in his early 40s. The man spoke better English than the little girl did, but his speech was still laced with a heavy Dutch accent.

"I thank you for the cigarettes and gifts you give to my daughter," he said to Bob and his crew. "I am Willem Cretier and this is my daughter Sussie," he continued. "I hope she is not bothering you by coming down here."

"No problem," Bob replied, noting that Willem seemed to be a sincere man. "I'm Bob Elliott."

The men shook hands and Bob introduced his crewmates to Willem. "This is my crew – Duke, George, Atchy and Conroy."

The crew had the motor compartments open to service the five Chrysler motors that powered the tank. Willem was fascinated at these engines mounted in a circle and running in unison on the same transmission

"Those are Chrysler engines," Willem commented. "I have never seen five of them working together like that. I am a mechanic and I used to be an agent for the Chrysler engines. Do you mind if I have a look at them?"

"Go ahead," replied Bob. "We can use all the help we can get."

Willem stood behind the tank and listened carefully to the engines running. Using his mechanical expertise, he determined which particular motor needed extra attention and exactly what was needed. He soon had all five engines working in perfect harmony.

Bob was impressed by Willem's abilities. "There are a lot of engines in our Army that could use your expertise," he told Willem. "Would you consider working for us while we're here to help get our equipment in order?"

"Yes," Willem replied. "I would like to do that. I have my own shop in Rossum, only six or seven kilometres from here, but I had to escape with my family from the Germans. If the Fort Garry men had not been here, we would have all been killed by now – my wife, my three children – all of us. We were working with the Underground for a long time and the Germans found out just over a month ago."

"I heard about the Underground. A very brave group," Bob said. "I'd like to hear more about that some day. I'll talk to our commanding officer about you, but I'm pretty sure he'll welcome the idea of a good mechanic on the team."

Bob wasted no time convincing his CO to hire Willem. After that, Willem and Sussie became a familiar sight near Bob's tank.

Kees and Gerard were not as inquisitive as Sussie. They spent their time playing with other children and each other. Sussie was more daring and had already made friends with some of the men from the Fort Garry regiment. She looked forward to meeting more of these people from another land and learning more about them. Like many of her countrymen, Sussie could not believe that young men from another country would come and save the Dutch people from their plight. Every day, she was grateful to them.

The CO was so impressed with Willem's mechanical abilities that he made Willem an honorary member of the 19th Field Regiment and even presented him with his own rum ration cup. This arrangement formed a special friendship between Bob and Willem that lasted for decades.

One day in mid-December when the weather was starting to turn cold, Willem was doing some extensive work on the motors of Bob's tank when he struck his hand hard with a hammer.

"Pot verdomme!" Willem yelled.

Bob thought that Willem's exclamation was some kind of Dutch cuss word, but he didn't inquire as to its meaning. Instead, Bob asked, "Are you okay?"

"It's okay," Willem replied. "I don't think I broke anything. It just hurts a lot right now."

Later that evening, Willem joined the soldiers for their nightly rum ration. Perhaps the pain from his injury was the catalyst that caused him to imbibe in the rum a little too much that night because by the time he headed for home, his soldier friends considered Willem to be fairly inebriated.

Willem staggered in the door of the Cretiers' humble living quarters and promptly passed out on the bed. Sussie and her brothers were worried that something was seriously wrong with their father. He had blood on his hand and didn't move from the moment he landed on the bed. Geert quickly discovered that Willem smelled of alcohol. She turned to her three concerned children and told them with considerable relief, "He is going to be alright. Just let him sleep. He'll be fine in the morning."

The next day, Willem woke with a terrible hangover and Geert told him how the children had reacted. "Well, you never know," she added. "You could have been shot. After all, we are still at war." Then she started to see the funny side of the situation and gave Willem a big hug and kiss. Bob and the tank crew also enjoyed a good laugh later when they learned of the children's reaction to their passed-out father.

* * * * *

The holding line along the Maas River wasn't anything like the intense fighting the Canadians had experienced on their way there from Juno Beach. Bob was thankful for that. This was nothing like the Scheldt estuary or the Walcheren Island battles. There were many hours when nothing much happened on their shift. The soldiers just sat around talking about everything from girlfriends they'd left behind to what they were going to do when this was all over and they returned to Canada. They also had plenty of time to visit with their new friends in Alphen.

On days when Bob and his crew were off duty, Willem invited them for supper to the farmhouse where he and his family were living. The Cretiers didn't have much space, but that didn't stop them from entertaining their new-found friends. They spent many enjoyable evenings this way, learning more of each other's languages.

"Dit is en coptje," Geert would say as she held up a cup.

"This is a cup," Bob would say in return, holding up his cup.

"Dit is en vork," Geert said as she held up a fork.

Before long, they were able to converse relatively well and spent many happy hours visiting.

For Sussie, these brave soldiers were very special. She loved visiting Bob's crew in particular. For one thing, these men were kind to her, and they gave her treats to bring home for herself and her brothers. Secondly, they allowed her to climb up in their tank, which was much more fun than her routine had been for the past few years of being careful with everything she said and did, or having to hide in her great aunt's cellar. She admired these soldiers and visited them every day.

Sussie often sat on top of Bob's tank and sang. With her beautiful voice and infectious smile, she soon became a star to the soldiers, singing the Dutch national anthem, the popular German love song 'Lili Marleen' and many other tunes. The Canadians taught her to sing 'O Canada' and decided that she should be their regiment's mascot and good-luck charm for the rest of the war.

One day, Bob decided to paint Sussie's name on the Sexton so that the luck she gave to him and his crew would go wherever they went. Upon seeing the beginning of Bob's paint job, Sussie protested mildly. "My name is not Suzy," she said. "It's Everdina."

Bob stood back from his artwork and looked at Sussie. "I've never heard that name before. Does it have an English equivalent?"

Sussie didn't know what an equivalent was, and when she was given an explanation of the word, she said she didn't know what Everdina would be in English either. Bob did some investigating of his own and learned that the English translation for Everdina was Evelyne. Bob thought that her real name would have more meaning than a nickname and, because he and his crew spoke English, the name should be written in English, so that was the name he painted on the tank – 'Evelyne.'

For Sussie, it was a great honour to have her name painted on a Canadian war tank, no matter how they spelled it!

* * * * *

One of the main combat duties for Bob's tank crew at Alphen was destroying the Germans' launching sites for their unmanned rocket bombs known as V1s and V2s. These lethal weapons were aimed at England, then launched and calculated to run out of fuel when they approached their target.

Canadian intelligence gathered information on the physical location of these sites to the north of the Waal River and passed it on to the artillery, which then attempted to destroy the targets. This was accomplished with devastating accuracy, much to the annoyance of the Germans who, in turn, tried to eliminate their attackers. The Germans also tried to confuse the Allies by frequently moving their launching sites. This game of cat and mouse continued from November 1944 until February 1945, when the final push into Germany was ordered.

One morning as Sussie approached Bob's tank, the holding line was under heavy fire from the Germans. "You shouldn't be down here when the Germans are shooting at us! It's too dangerous!" Bob yelled as he ran to Sussie, picked her up and lifted her up onto the tank. "Get inside," he ordered. "You'll be safe in there."

So Sussie climbed into the tank with the crew. "Here, you'd better put these on," Bob said, handing her some earmuffs.

None of the crew spoke to her. They were too busy loading, aiming and firing the big gun while Sussie just sat there feeling guilty from Bob's scolding. She soon felt better after chewing some gum that Bob gave her, though. She realized that he was only concerned for her safety.

The 25-pound gun sounded incredibly loud from inside the tank when it was firing, but that didn't bother Sussie. She thought it was great to be a part of this war. She felt like she was part of the tank crew now, and being in a tank that was shooting back at the Germans for all the wicked things they had done to her country gave her a feeling of power she had not previously experienced.

That day, Everdina (Sussie) Cretier became the youngest soldier fighting in Alphen. She could hardly believe her good luck!

There were thousands of Canadian soldiers stationed along the holding line at the Maas River during the winter of 1944-1945 and their compassion for the starving Dutch people was unanimous. Most of the soldiers refused to take their full rations so that there would be plenty of leftovers for the local residents. Some even badgered their commanding officers to get the Allied governments to do something about this travesty of human suffering. They finally made some headway on that front and food supplies were distributed, not only for the liberated sections in the Netherlands but to the German-occupied zone of the Netherlands as well. This was achieved by making a deal with the Germans to allow Allied bombers to fly into these areas and drop thousands of food packages.

Despite the Canadians' concentrated efforts to destroy the German launching sites for their V1 flying bombs and V2 rockets, these weapons were still launched towards England from just across the river at the rate of at least 100 a day. On a cool morning in December 1944, Sussie was fetching a small covered pail of milk from a local farm when she heard one of the V1 flying bombs nearby. It was approaching at a low altitude and its motor was cutting in and out, which told her that this particular bomb would not be going much further.

She looked in the direction of the river but she couldn't see the bomb. Then she turned and looked in another direction and saw that the bomb was heading right at her. Then its engine stopped altogether!

Sussie quickly looked for a place to hide. The only protection she could see was a large pile of used bedding straw mixed with animal manure that had been cleaned out of a barn. She tried to climb into the awful smelling pile and had just buried her head and shoulders in it when the bomb exploded and took out an entire block of the town of Alphen.

The shock wave from the blast lifted Sussie's body off the ground. It felt like some invisible giant hand had slapped her. There was screaming coming from the farmhouse nearby. Someone there had been hurt. Sussie trembled so much that she couldn't move. She couldn't feel anything. The blast had numbed her whole body and she didn't know if she had been injured or not.

Geert had heard the huge explosion. She knew that, based on the direction of the sound, Sussie was in danger. Geert ran out of the house to see if she could see her daughter or find someone to help her find Sussie. A Canadian soldier they knew only as Ned, who was a special dispatch rider in the Canadian Army, was passing the farmhouse just then on his motorbike. Geert flagged him down and begged him to find her daughter.

"She was somewhere near where that bomb exploded," Geert told him.

"Don't worry," Ned assured her. "I will find her and bring her home." He gunned his motorbike and went searching for Sussie. A few minutes later, Ned found Sussie in a state of shock, standing near the pile of manure and straw, covered in dirt and manure and still feeling numb from the explosion.

"Are you okay?" Ned asked as he stopped the bike near her. Sussie wasn't sure yet, so she just nodded, unable to speak.

"Here, give me the milk," Ned ordered as he took the still-intact covered milk pail from Sussie and placed it on the seat between his thighs. "Now, get on the motorbike behind me. I'm taking you home. Your mother is really worried about you."

Sussie had never had a ride on a motorcycle before and her fear from the bomb blast was suddenly replaced by a surge of excitement as Ned wound the throttle of the big bike and drove her quickly home. The rest of her family was waiting anxiously for her return. Geert was so pleased to see her daughter safe and sound that she hugged Ned and thanked him for finding her Sussie, then hugged her daughter and checked her out for injuries. There was nothing broken and no severe bruising. Just the evil-smelling residue from the life-saving manure pile.

"I think I'm going to lie down for awhile," Sussie said suddenly. "I don't feel good." The reality of her close call with death was starting to sink in. The numbness was gone now, but the ringing in her ears and the smell of spent explosive from the bomb still lingering in her nostrils left her somewhat nauseated. Perhaps a good sleep would help her feel better.

Many of the people of Alphen were killed and scores were injured on that terrible day. The Canadian soldiers did everything they could to help find survivors, clean up the mess and bury the dead. Everything stopped on the battle lines while their Army ambulances and field hospital facilities sprang into action to tend to the wounded.

The selfless actions of these soldiers on that day further cemented a relationship between the Netherlands and Canada that will last forever. Never before had an Army done so much for a people in the aftermath of a terrible oppression. They liberated them from their German captors, fed them to the best of their ability and gave them back their dignity. The Dutch people reciprocated by opening their homes to these young men from a far-away land who had willingly risked their lives to come and save them from a terrible oppression. An eternal bond was formed.

For Sussie, that close encounter helped her develop a particularly acute sense of hearing for V1s and V2s. From then on, she was able to pinpoint their location from the moment they were launched. This unique ability enabled her to become an early warning device for the Canadian soldiers. They used Sussie's information to locate the launching ramps. Before the Germans could move the ramps, the Canadians sent a hail of shells in that direction to cut off further bomb attacks.

The men of the Fort Garry Regiment had given Sussie a beret with their regimental badge on it shortly after she had arrived in Alphen. Sussie wore it often and was even more convinced that she was now a member of the Canadian Army when Bob's crew sewed two stripes on the arm of her torn green coat, just like she had seen on the sleeves of some of their jackets. One stripe was for lance corporal and the other was for the Canadian Army. She also had the Fort Garry Horse Regiment badge on her left sleeve.

When Sussie got home that day from her visit with the soldiers, Willem noticed her new strips of cloth.

"What's that you have on your sleeve?" he asked her.

"I've got stripes now!" Sussie happily replied.

"So, what does that mean?" her father inquired.

"I don't know, but it makes me one of the tank crew," said a smiling Sussie.

Geert had been sitting at the table watching this interchange. With a smile on her face, she slowly shook her head and wondered what her little girl would come home with next.

One other day while Sussie was visiting Bob and his troops, Bob mentioned that she needed to "keep a low profile" when the captain of the regiment came around. Sussie didn't know exactly what Bob meant by that comment, but after it was explained to her, she was careful to stay out of the way of the commanding officers.

Sussie spent as much time as she could with Bob's crew. They made her feel very special, always taking time to talk to her except when they were busy shooting at the enemy. Even then, she was usually in the tank with them hoping that every shell they fired would wreak some devastating havoc on the Germans. Sussie had no fear of being in a combat zone, but she was still terrified of the rats in the old barn.

"What is a whore?" she asked Bob one day while he was busy with tank maintenance.

"Who told you that?" Bob asked, stopping what he was doing and showing immediate concern.

"Duke did," she replied.

"Duke!" Bob yelled. "I want to talk to you!"

Duke came around the tank to where Bob was standing. "What's the problem?" he asked nonchalantly.

"I'll tell you what the problem is," Bob scolded. "Why would you teach this young girl a bad word? She doesn't need to know what a whore is. These folk have been through hell and need our protection. Don't you ever do that again!"

Bob's intensity must have gotten through to Duke because he did not make that mistake a second time.

It was at that moment that Sussie knew Bob Elliott was much more than a good friend. He was her guardian angel. She knew that as long as she stayed close to him, nothing could harm her. From that moment on, Sussie became Bob's little shadow, following him wherever he went.

Sometimes when Bob went to visit families in Alphen, Sussie followed him and sat outside on the front step of the house where Bob was visiting. Minutes or hours later, whenever Bob came out after his visit, Sussie would quietly ask him, "What took you so long?"

This amused Bob considerably. Part of him enjoyed having an extra shadow, especially one with such innocence and such a brave heart.

Sussie's routine during those days rarely varied. She fetched a small pail of milk every morning from the farm where she almost lost her life to the bomb. Then she hurried to do any other chores she was asked to do so she could go visit with her favourite group of soldiers. At mealtimes, she waited at the Army mess hall for any leftovers that the cook would give her to take home. To her delight, she never had to go home empty-handed. The Canadians always found something for her.

About every two weeks, a care package arrived from Canada for Bob and every few days a package came to him from Auntie Nan. There were cakes, cookies, candy, chocolate, and sometimes a small gift inside, and there was always a letter included from the sender carrying the latest news from Calgary or Paisley. Bob invariably wrote back every time he received one of these packages to express his gratitude and inform his mother and aunt that he was okay.

Although Kees and Gerard didn't spend as much time with these Canadian soldiers as Sussie did, they seemed to have a special internal detection device to inform them of the moment Bob's care packages arrived. There were always three pairs of youthful eyes watching Bob unwrap his parcels with obvious anticipation. One memorable package contained a flashlight, something that Sussie and her brothers had never seen. The beam of light emanating from the strange tube-like object was fascinating to the three Cretier children. The austere life they had lived under the Germans hadn't lent itself to luxuries and this flashlight had to be one of the most fascinating things they'd ever encountered. Of course, the candy, chocolate and chewing gum that Bob always gave them ran a close second.

The farmer who owned the barn that Bob and his crew had converted into their bunkhouse gave Bob a pair of wooden shoes one day. The farmer had made some woven straw insoles for the shoes as well. Bob found these shoes not only warm and comfortable, but convenient to slip into when he had to walk down to the tank. There were no laces to do up, which was a welcome change from his regulation army boots. Bob had heard of Dutch clogs but never would have dreamed they could be so useful.

"There's a road show coming here to entertain the troops," Bob said to Sussie about two weeks before Christmas 1944. "How would you and your brothers like to go to it with us?"

Sussie looked a little puzzled, "What's a road show?" she asked, trying to picture how a road would do a show.

"There will be singers and comedians, people who tell funny jokes, maybe a little drama. It's kind of like going to the theatre, with actors and such."

"Oh," Sussie replied. "Okay, we'll go."

The show was held in a big barn and the entire community of Alphen had been invited. The Cretier children sat with Bob, Duke and George. They had a great time! The antics of the female clown made Sussie and her brothers laugh uncontrollably. The clown was wearing an alarm clock for a wristwatch! At that moment, the horrors of the war had been forgotten and the only important thing was the hilarious clown dancing in front of them with a gigantic wristwatch on her arm.

The live music was fascinating and the singers were also fabulous. Sussie had a wonderful evening and felt so privileged to be there with her favourite Canadian soldiers.

Not long after that, Bob's Christmas package arrived from his mother. It was lovingly wrapped in cotton cloth. The package contained his favourite Christmas treat, a block of fruitcake. Beautiful homemade fruitcake. To Bob's dismay, a strange smell wafted up at him when he opened the parcel. The chocolate bars were okay and the cigarettes had survived due to waterproof packaging, but the fruitcake did not fare as well.

Apparently a fire had broken out in the hold of the ship that had delivered his parcel and everything had to be sprayed with pyrene, a chemical used at the time to extinguish fires. Bob tried letting his fruitcake sit on a shelf for a few days to air out, but this did not help. The awful taste of pyrene wouldn't leave, so he had to eventually throw out his precious gift.

Above: Minister de Jong's house during wartime. Willem Cretier hid in the eaves to avoid capture by the Nazis.

Right: The modern-day Rossum bridge, over which the Cretiers crossed to safety.

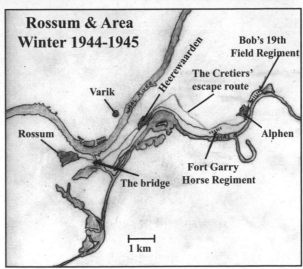

**Rossum & Area
Winter 1944-1945**

Bob's 19th
Field Regiment

The Cretiers'
escape route

Heerewaarden

Varik

Alphen

Rossum

Fort Garry
Horse Regiment

The bridge

1 km

Left: V1 flying bomb on display at the Musée de l'Armée in Paris, France.
Photo – www.wikipedia.org

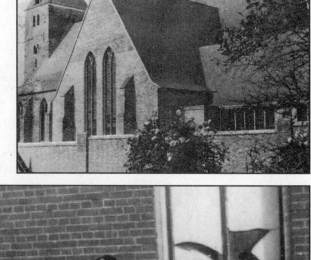

Right: Roman Catholic Church in Alphen on the Maas, Netherlands, 1944-1945.

Ten-year-old Sussie Cretier wearing her Fort Garry Horse Regiment beret and her torn green coat with the stripes sewn on the sleeve by Bob's crew, in front of an abandoned grocery store in Alphen, Netherlands, 1944.

CHAPTER NINE

The little coat

"So what are we going to do for Sussie for Christmas?" Bob asked his crew a few days later. "She is our lucky charm and we should give her something."

"She could sure use some new clothes," one of the men suggested. "The ones she's wearing now have pretty much had it."

Their conversation turned to other things for awhile but eventually came back to Sussie and her Christmas gift. "New clothes are a great idea, so let's do that," Bob commented. "She badly needs a coat, so we should get her that to begin with, but why don't we get her some other things to go with the coat, too? Maybe some shoes, a sweater and hat and scarf?"

The men agreed.

"Okay, we know what we want to give her," Duke noted, "but how are we going to get all these things? There's nothing in the stores around here. The Germans made sure of that."

The crew fell silent while they pondered this predicament.

"I hear that some of the locals have been making clothes out of wool Army blankets," George observed. "Maybe we could do that, too."

"Good idea. Yeah, a really good idea," the others agreed.

"Okay, that's great," Atchy said. "We can find a good Army blanket no problem, but who's going to make the clothes?"

"Hey, Bob, did you bring your sewing machine with you?" Duke joked.

"If I had, I would have sewed up the ends of your German souvenir scarf so it wouldn't get so frayed," Bob shot back.

Like every good idea, making it become a reality had a few stumbling blocks along the way, but this group of brave men who had whupped the Germans halfway across Europe weren't about to give up. No sir, they would make this happen. They resolved to see it materialize and also agreed that this project had to be perfect for their regiment's good-luck charm.

The men spread their idea among some of the other 174 soldiers in their regiment along that row of war machines, to see if any of them had ideas on how to create clothing for their Sussie. Many of the other soldiers were happy to pitch in.

Sussie had become a symbol of what this war was all about. She was a physical reminder of why these young men had made so many sacrifices – of their youth, their safety and, in some cases, their lives – to free these oppressed people from the Nazi regime. They would all suffer for years to come from the trauma of this war, but people like Sussie would remain in their minds and make all of the pain and nightmares somewhat more bearable.

"There's an old seamstress who lives up on the dyke," one of the men said. "I'll bet she could make a coat for Sussie."

"Two of us are going on leave for a few days to Paris," said another. "We could take up a collection and get the shoes, a scarf and maybe a sweater."

Bob was pleased with these ideas and thought they were ready to put their plan into action when another stumbling block came along. Sussie's shoe size was a problem. A secret study would have to be undertaken without her knowledge. They couldn't ask any of her family. It wasn't that they didn't trust the Cretiers. They just didn't want Sussie or her family to know what they were planning.

George had an idea. "Why don't we just measure her footprints? There's enough mud around for her to leave some here." This solution was so practical that the rest of the crew wondered why they hadn't thought of it first.

So a collection was taken and the money was sent to Paris with the two soldiers fortunate enough to get a break from their military duties. A good wool Army blanket was taken to the seamstress with the simple instructions that she was to make a coat for a 10-year-old girl and a pair of pants as well if there was enough fabric.

"Buttons. The seamstress needs buttons for the coat," Bob reported back to his crew shortly after they had put in their order. "We could each donate a button off our uniforms until we have enough."

So several soldiers each donated a button and all the components were soon in the hands of the seamstress to turn the idea of the little coat into reality.

The men who had gone to Paris returned with a nice pair of leather shoes, a sweater and a scarf. They knew these items would go well with the beret that the Fort Garry Regiment had given to Sussie during her first month in Alphen. Members of Bob's crew picked up the long-sleeved little coat from the seamstress and were pleased to see that she had also created matching pants out of the wool blanket's fabric. Years later, the soldiers would still marvel at how the seamstress had sewn both a coat and pants which ended up fitting Sussie exactly, without ever having measured the child!

Christmas was still a week away and there was a buzz of excitement coursing through the regiment. Many soldiers had heard about the coat and the men on the line near Bob's tank were anticipating Sussie's reaction when she opened the parcel they had so lovingly assembled for her.

Snow fell during the last week leading up to Christmas Day. Lots of snow. The temperatures dropped to below zero. The troops had no antifreeze for their tanks or vehicles so they had to start the machines every two hours and run them for 10 minutes to avoid frozen radiators.

"It looks like we got Sussie the right things for Christmas," one of the men commented, his breath making steam clouds in the cold winter air.

At daybreak on Christmas morning 1944, some enemy activity was observed. About 200 German soldiers were loading a fleet of small boats on the other side of the Waal River. The Canadians couldn't determine the nature of the cargo being stowed but decided to take no chances. A barrage of 25-pound shells was soon aimed at the flotilla, eventually sinking every boat.

"That's a Christmas parcel Jerry won't forget in a hurry!" Bob observed with a tone of satisfaction.

It was while this altercation was in progress that Sussie walked by Bob's tank on her way back from getting the daily milk for her family. One of the crew spotted her.

"Sussie is here!" he exclaimed.

"Okay! Quit firing while we give her the coat!" Bob ordered. They couldn't leave their position, but jumped off the tank just long enough to give Sussie her gift.

"Hey, Sussie!" Bob called. "Come over here! We've got something for you!"

Sussie put down the pail she was carrying and went to see what was happening.

One of the men handed her a big parcel. "This is just something for you for Christmas," Bob said.

Sussie couldn't believe her eyes when she opened the package and saw a beautiful pair of leather shoes, a pretty light blue sweater, a scarf, a pair of pants and the most wonderful coat she had ever seen in her life. This little coat wasn't the same colour as the uniforms the Canadian soldiers were wearing, but it had the same buttons on it. It was perfect!

"Oh, thank you! Thank you so much!" she exclaimed as she gave each of Bob's crew members a hug. "I'm going to put these on right now!"

The soldiers returned to their posts and continued demolishing the German activity on the other side of the river. It was a shame that most of the Canadian troops stationed along that holding line missed seeing Sussie at that moment. They were too busy fighting the Germans to share in the excitement of the little Dutch girl who had just received the best Christmas gift she could have imagined.

Sussie was so excited with her new clothes that she picked up her milk pail and walked straight home to show her mother.

Geert was sitting by the farmhouse window looking out at the cold but sunny Christmas morning. There, walking down the road toward the house, she saw a beautiful young girl who was so well dressed that tears started to well up in Geert's eyes.

"Look at how beautifully dressed that young girl is," Geert called to Willem. "I wish we could dress our Sussie like that." Not being able to supply her children with the necessities of life had been difficult for Geert to accept.

Then the door of the house opened and in came the most excited Sussie that Geert and Willem had seen in a long time.

"Look, Mom! Look what Bob and his crew gave me!" Sussie said excitedly, showing off her new outfit.

Sussie thought her mother was going to pass out. Tears were rolling down her mother's cheeks.

These were tears of happiness, though. Geert could not believe that it had been her own little girl that she had seen coming down the road in those beautiful clothes!

Willem, meanwhile, was speechless. All he could do was stare in wonder at the precious gifts the Canadian soldiers had given his daughter.

"Let me look at you," Geert said as she released her daughter from a long embrace.

Sussie paraded for her mother with a smile on her face that suggested she was the happiest girl in the whole world at that moment.

"You look so beautiful!" Geert couldn't contain the joy she felt for her daughter. Her tears just kept coming for the next few minutes.

"Isn't this wonderful, Mom? Isn't this just the best thing that ever happened? I love the Canadian soldiers! They have been so good to us. I wish that some day we can do something good for them, too."

Kees and Gerard were amazed and happy for their sister as well. Seeing her that happy made them feel happy, too. They were later treated to their own stock of chocolate and candy from the Canadians for Christmas, but nothing could equal the joy they saw on their sister's face at that moment.

As Willem watched this historic event in his family's life, he wore a smile on his face and gratitude in his heart. If he wasn't careful, he would also be crying tears of happiness, he thought to himself. It was a moment of pure joy to see his little girl so excited with her Christmas gifts from the Canadian soldiers.

Later that day, the soldiers were in total agreement that the Christmas dinner they ate in the Canadian Army mess hall that evening was the best meal they'd eaten since enlisting. There was duck a l'orange with all the trimmings and plenty of food for everyone.

Sussie had gone to the mess hall, wearing her new clothes, to see if there were any leftovers. The kitchen staff had prepared a huge dish of food for her to take home. It was so heavy that she could barely carry it. That Christmas meal was thoroughly enjoyed by all of the Cretiers.

Sussie was so happy, she could have just burst! She not only had her new clothes, a good meal for her loving family, and some wonderful soldier friends, but she and the other people of Alphen knew that soon they would all have their freedom, and that would be the best present of all.

* * * * *

The following week passed without incident and New Year's Eve arrived. There were no fireworks available so, at midnight, the Canadians decided to give the Germans their own brand of fireworks. They sent a barrage of shells across the river to celebrate the beginning of 1945.

Tuesday of each week was the designated day for the soldiers to clean their rifles and shine their boots and brass buttons. Now that Sussie had her outfit with the Army buttons along with her Fort Garry beret, she joined the soldiers in this ritual. She would have loved to clean a rifle, too, but Bob wouldn't allow it. Every Tuesday after that Christmas Day, Sussie polished her Army buttons with the men and played the part of a soldier.

Sometimes she joined the men in the mess hall for a meal. One day, she was standing in line with George and Duke when the soldier behind the counter asked her, "Since when did you become a soldier?"

Before Sussie could think of anything to say, Duke replied for her, "Since a long time. Now load up her plate." So Sussie's plate was filled and she joined the men at a long table to eat.

Every evening, Sussie hung up her little coat and gazed at it lovingly as though it was her most treasured possession in the whole world. She vowed she would keep it in good condition for the rest of her life, even after she had grown too big to wear it.

It was the most special gift she had ever received.

CHAPTER TEN

Germany

Another month passed for Bob and his crew before anything major occurred. The Canadians routinely took potshots at the German military locations but, for the most part, enjoyed a reasonably benign location in the war. For Bob, Atchy, George, Duke and Conroy, it was a time of alternating between military obligations and enjoyable visits with the Cretier family.

Stationed along the Maas River since early November 1944, the Allies had suffered very few casualties while inflicting painful losses on the Germans. On February 3, 1945, Bob's regiment was given its orders to relocate to a new position in a forest near Nijmegen, about 50 miles northeast of Alphen, close to the German border.

For the people of Alphen, the last three months had been a wonderful time of friendship with these young soldiers who had come to liberate their country. On their final day in Alphen, almost every person in the town lined the street to watch their heroes leave.

The Cretiers had risen early that morning to join the cheering crowd. After several unsuccessful attempts to find Sussie, the rest of the Cretiers went to the main street to say goodbye to their Canadian friends and wish them good luck. There, while in the crowd, Geert's gaze became fixated on a soldier in the turret of the lead tank.

'That soldier looks rather small to be a part of an army,' Geert thought. Then she looked again.

"That little soldier looks just like Sussie!" Geert exclaimed aloud.

As the tank drew closer, Geert had a better view. "Oh, my Lord! That is Sussie! What is she doing up there?"

Both Geert and Willem were quite amused at the sight of their brave little soldier girl. There she was, riding in Bob's tank, wearing her little coat and her regimental beret with its Canadian badge, and looking like she was ready to go into battle and defeat the Germans.

Sussie had made a deal with Bob that she would leave the tank once they got to the edge of town. That way, she could ride with her favourite crew one last time. It was so much fun being a part of this great Army. Sussie knew she was going to miss them all after they were gone.

As they had arranged, Bob dropped Sussie off at the edge of Alphen and the tanks headed on for Nijmegen.

The Canadian Army's new location was only three miles from the German border. The soldiers were confined to the immediate vicinity of their equipment and all around them in the dense forest, Bob could hear the movements of a large number of armoured vehicles and infantry.

'I wonder when they'll let us know what's happening,' Bob wondered. 'Something big must be coming up.'

The soldiers didn't have long to wait. Within four hours of arriving, a letter from Allied Command was read aloud. It sounded a lot like the letter that had been read to them on their trip across the English Channel en route to Juno Beach.

"Once again, the eyes of the Free World are upon you," the officer addressing their regiment announced. "Tomorrow morning, you will be attacking the enemy in his homeland and you can expect him to raise a stubborn defence. We know we are experienced, have good troops and equipment. With this battle, we will end the war. Good luck and God bless you all."

'Will this be as bad as the Juno Beach landing?' Bob wondered. 'It won't be fun, but I can't see it being anything like Juno Beach. The Germans have suffered heavy losses on all fronts, so we should win this one. I guess this is their homeland though, so they won't be real happy with us being on their turf.'

Bob's feelings wavered from positive to negative and back again. 'In the final analysis, we have a job to do,' he decided. 'We came to free Europe from Hitler and, by golly, we've pretty much done it. Just this last push and it's all over.'

At 4:30 a.m. on February 8, 1945, Bob's sleep was shattered by the deafening sound of 2,000 guns and rockets firing on the German border. At first, Bob thought the Germans had developed some new kind of demoralizing weapon similar to the Moaning Minnie mortar rockets that screamed louder and louder as they fell to earth, scaring the devil out of anyone in the immediate vicinity, but ultimately causing very little damage. Then he realized that the nearest rockets were being launched 16 at a time from a position only a hundred yards behind his tank.

This was the first time he had been that close to the launching of these weapons. The sound from those launches was the loudest thing he and his crew had experienced so far, even louder than their 25-pound field gun when they were sitting right next to it as it fired.

"That's gotta be the worst wake-up call I've ever had," Bob yelled over the roar of the screaming rockets. "They could have let us know what to expect."

His crew was struggling to achieve full awareness.

"I guess they figured they would only have to wake the rocket crew up and the noise would do the job on the rest of us," Duke commented.

George joined in. "I'll go make some breakfast. I think we'll be moving soon." George started up the gasoline cooker and fried up some sausages and beans to start their day.

George was right. Within the hour, orders to mobilize were distributed.

"Well, boys, I guess this is it. We're going into Germany," Bob said as he fired up the tank engines. "Are you ready for this?"

"Are you kidding?" Atchy said, "This is what we've been waiting for!"

At the outset of the final battle to defeat the Nazis, Bob's regiment, the 19th Field Regiment supported the 53rd Welsh Division in attempts to break through the extensive German line of defence. This line, known as the Siegfried line, encompassed the whole of Germany a few miles in from the border. It was designed to repel any Allied invasion. The German soldiers who manned it were told there would be no surrender.

The area from the border to the Siegfried line was littered with mines and booby traps of every kind, intended to inflict as many casualties as possible on an invading army before that army reached the line. The most effective and annoying device was the shoe mine. When stepped on, these small wooden boxes about the size of a small shoebox immobilized a man by blowing off his legs. It would not necessarily kill him but it certainly put him out of action. The Germans had placed thousands of these nasty anti-personnel weapons throughout their perimeter and Bob greatly admired the minesweeping teams who cleared the way for the rest of the soldiers.

It seemed that every time a major battle was fought in this war, it was accompanied by heavy rain, and this one was no different. The inclement weather did more to hamper the advance of the Allies than the mines did. With more mud than one could possibly imagine in this border area, vehicles bogged down and tempers flared. Advance was unbelievably slow.

While the unfavourable conditions caused a great deal of difficulty, it was a blessing in disguise for the Allies. The rain washed off the two inches of soil covering the shoe mines, which enabled safe removal of almost 100 per cent of the mines and saved the infantrymen who had to walk through those areas.

Part of the Canadian advance route was through the Reichswald Forest, where the soldiers made good use of the plentiful deer population. A few tasty meals of fresh venison went down well with the men and were a welcome diversion from their Army rations.

There were other highlights during this, the final battle for freedom. Around the middle of February, Bob's regiment captured a small German village when Duke, the best gun loader Bob had ever seen, disappeared from the tank. Duke's nerves had become more than a little frayed from all the action in the war and he occasionally enjoyed a drink or two to settle his nerves and keep up the fight. Liquor was hard to find during full battle engagement, however, and Duke was feeling the strain.

As the rest of the crew were searching for Duke that day, they passed a church. Up on the steps, they saw a figure dressed in a long purple robe emerge from the front doors with a bottle of wine in his hand. They had found Duke. And Duke had found the local priest's communion wine from which he had obviously been imbibing.

Duke stood there at the top of the steps, made a rather over-emphasized Sign of the Cross and loudly proclaimed, "Bless you, my brothers!"

Duke's euphoria was only temporary, though. A few days after that incident, Bob realized he would have to get his good friend out of this stressful situation before Duke went past the point of no return. Bob requested a transfer for Duke, which was granted. A few days later, Bob saw Duke driving an ammunition truck. He pulled his tank in close to the truck and signalled for Duke to stop.

Bob turned off the noisy tank and teased Duke. "So you figure driving a mobile bomb is easier on the nerves?"

"You know what?" Duke replied, "I get a good night's sleep now. I could never get to sleep in that damn tank. Me and lack of sleep don't get along too well."

"Well, you sure look better. Your new job must be agreeing with you. All the best of luck to you and we'll see you at the end of the road, if not before," Bob said as he fired up his tank. "Better get back to work before the Germans think we've quit!"

By February 27, 1945, the repatriation of Italy was complete, allowing the Canadian 1st and 5th Divisions to join forces with the rest of their Army to liberate the northern Netherlands and help deliver the final blow to Germany. Shortly after crossing the Rhine River on the way to Berlin, Bob's regiment was relieved by the forces from Italy. His tank crew was pulled out of the combat line and sent to Tilburg, Netherlands. This was about 40 miles from Antwerp, the major Belgian port where the incoming supplies for the Canadian Forces were landing.

Since they would now be close to new supplies, Bob and his crew had more reason to share the items they carried with them. They had some pork on board their tank, which they had commandeered from a German farm the day before. They gave a hind quarter of the pork and half a loaf of white bread to a Dutch family in dire need of food. The elderly lady who accepted the food was so grateful that Bob thought she might squeeze the life out of him with her big hug. She and Bob exchanged addresses and he kept in touch with them for many years after the war.

The crew's two-week stay in Tilburg included some much-needed rest and relaxation, but it was mainly a time to refit the tanks with mud cleats and perform some mechanical maintenance. It was at times like this that Bob wished they had Willem with them to tune the motors. The engines had never run better than when he had used his magical touch on them.

The crews in Tilburg were also instructed to brush up on their rifle and parade ground drill. Bob had his crew out in the street going through their paces – marching, presenting arms, slope arms, the whole routine. At the end of one of these exercises, just as he had dismissed the men, a Dutch girl who lived in the house where they were billeted, approached Bob and asked, "Why don't you have to do the drill? You just stand there and give orders. Go and get your rifle!" she ordered.

After Bob retrieved his weapon, the girl proceeded to give Bob his rifle drill by repeating, word for word, every command he had spoken to his men. Bob humoured her by obeying her orders while the rest of his crew cheered her on.

Their sojourn at Tilburg came to an end in mid-March when the 19th Field Regiment was ordered back into battle, working their way north up the Dutch-German border, alternating back and forth from the Netherlands to Germany. On April 4, after a tough battle clearing the Germans out of the Dutch town of Almelo, just 12 miles from the German border in northeast Netherlands, Bob unexpectedly became an assistant midwife.

The battery captain had taken up residence in a local house, establishing a command post there. Bob was receiving orders in that house when the woman who lived there decided it was time to have her baby. There was no doctor anywhere to be found so Captain Stirling rolled up his sleeves, started giving Bob orders and proceeded to deliver a healthy baby boy! This was the first time Bob had seen a baby born. It was very exciting to have been a part of this marvellous event. After having been instrumental in the demise of countless enemy soldiers, Bob felt elated at having helped bring a new life into the world.

Although Bob tried later to keep in touch with the Dutch people he encountered during the war, this particular family moved away from Almelo and left no forwarding address. The only information Bob found out was that the baby boy had been named Bastiaan.

As each Dutch town was relinquished from the iron grip of the Nazis, the Dutch people greeted their liberators with such fervour that the soldiers were overwhelmed. These long-oppressed people lined the streets, waving their flags and displaying their thanks for being delivered from their bondage, even though the Germans were still close at hand. They were so grateful to be rid of their captors that they pointed out every German sniper and asked the Allies to destroy every building still occupied by the enemy.

It was here that Bob captured a high-ranking German officer along with his Mercedes Benz car and all his belongings. Among the items this important prisoner carried was a substantial supply of cigars. Bob decided those items would look better in his kitbag than with the German, so he confiscated the cigars and turned the rest of the German's belongings over to the soldiers taking care of prisoners.

A few days later, Bob was sitting on the tank enjoying some quiet time when he lit up one of those stogies. The first few quiet puffs were quite enjoyable. Then George came bursting out of the tank with a submachine gun in his hands.

"There's a German out there somewhere!" George exclaimed, "I can smell him! I'm going to get him!"

Bob grinned at his overzealous crewman and showed George the cigar he was smoking. "German cigar," Bob said. "I got them off that officer we caught earlier."

"Oh," George said, feeling somewhat foolish. "You really had me going there. Those cigars have a smell all their own, and that smell is German."

"Well, you can relax," Bob said quietly. "The only Germans anywhere near here are behind barbed wire. We cleared them all out today. But you'll get your chance to use that gun tomorrow."

* * * * *

On May 5, 1945, the German Army in the Netherlands officially surrendered. The Dutch people celebrated this event all over their country. The fighting was still going on in Germany, however.

On the morning of May 7, while Bob's regiment was advancing on the city of Oldenburg, one of the Canadian soldiers reported having heard a BBC radio broadcast announcing that the war was going to end the next day.

"I don't know if I believe that," Bob said as they kept firing on German troop positions. However, at 6:00 p.m. that evening, the order came down to cease fire. At 8:00 a.m. the next morning, the official ceasefire order was received.

Berlin had fallen, Hitler was dead and the Germans had surrendered.

The war was over!

The war was over?

Bob had a hard time grasping this turn of events. The landing at Normandy, the capture of Caen and Falaise, the trip through Belgium, the Scheldt estuary and Walcheren Island, the winter holding lines at Alphen and finally defeating the Germans in their homeland had all been experiences he would never forget. And now it was all over.

After pondering the fact that he had made it through alive, Bob reflected again on the previous 11 months. The landing at Juno Beach, the tragic loss of three crew members when they were hit by a mortar bomb, the fact that the three survivors of that original crew, George, Atchy and himself had come through the rest of the battles unscathed.

'So what happens now? Where do I go from here?'

These questions raced through Bob's mind as he realized he hadn't really expected to be alive at the end of the war.

On May 8, 1945, the day of the official end to the war in Europe, Bob and his crew were in their tank, parked in a farmer's field in Germany. Bob was looking for some chickens that his crew could eat when an elderly German woman came out of the farmhouse. She had been hiding in the basement for six days. When Bob spoke to her, she told him about her two sons who had been killed on the Russian front while serving in the German Army. She showed Bob photos of her sons dressed in their uniforms and wearing the Iron Cross, the German medal of honour.

'What a terrible waste of life,' Bob thought as he considered the war and gazed at the handsome young men in the photos.

'And it didn't solve anything. Why couldn't the political leaders just sit down and talk things out, and settle their differences in a civilized manner? Thousands of years of wars and misery and the human race still hadn't learned a darn thing!'

A few days later, a memo came from Allied Command offering a chance to go home immediately. The catch was that if a soldier chose to take that offer, he had only 30 days at home before he would have to go to the Pacific where the war with the Japanese was still raging. The alternative was to wait in Europe, wherever the Army assigned him, until transportation home to Canada could be arranged. That could take anywhere from six months to a year. Bob didn't have to think about that choice for very long. He felt he had done his part and would not sign up for any more duty. He was so sure of this that he wrote a short poem on the subject:

> A soldier with five years service
> Has few troubles on his mind
> He volunteers for nothing
> And is very hard to find
>
> — Bob Elliott, 1945

On May 11, after three days of cleaning and painting the tank, Bob was on his way to Scotland for 10 days of long-service leave.

He sure had a lot to tell Uncle Archie and Auntie Nan.

CHAPTER ELEVEN

Going home to Rossum

After the Canadians left Alphen, Sussie didn't go to the front line nearly as much. The British Army had taken over responsibility for the security of the people of Alphen, and while the locals appreciated the soldiers being there, they didn't make friends with them as they had with the Canadians. The British troops only stayed a month and then Belgian soldiers took over. The Cretiers had no contact with those troops either.

Instead of going to visit the soldiers, Sussie just spent her time playing with her brothers. Her whole family was waiting for the day when the war was behind them and they could all go home.

Willem's employment as tank maintenance mechanic ended when the Canadian soldiers left Alphen. He immediately put out the word through the Underground network that he would go anywhere in the freed zone of the Netherlands for work. He was told that the town of Tilburg, in its bid to rebuild, needed a good mechanic to bring the town's public transportation system back into service. Within a week, Willem was offered the job and he gladly accepted.

This new job created another obstacle for the Cretier family to overcome. Tilburg was 45 kilometres from Alphen and Willem's only means of transportation was a bicycle. This meant he could only be with his family on weekends. Lady Luck must have been with Willem for this problem because he only had to make that gruelling bicycle ride one time. A man named Mr. Henket, who was legal advisor to the town of Tilburg, heard of Willem's plight and decided to do something about it. He procured a brand new Indian Scout motorcycle, probably through Army surplus, and presented this prize to Willem. The motorbike was still in its crate.

With his new faster mode of transportation, Willem felt as though the clouds of oppression had lifted and the beautiful sunlight of freedom had shone through for his family. He not only had an income, he now had the means to travel to and from his new job and be home more often than he had anticipated.

This arrangement continued until May 5, 1945, when Willem arrived home and happily announced to his family, "The war is over! The Germans have surrendered and we can go home to Rossum!"

This was the moment they had long awaited. With smiling faces and joy in their hearts, the Cretiers gathered up their few belongings, thanked the farmer and his wife for giving them a place to call home, and headed back to their house in Rossum.

Their journey back to Rossum was not without peril, though.

During their retreat, the Germans had laid down many landmines and thousands of booby traps which killed many more Dutch people before these weapons could all be found and destroyed. The Cretiers had to pass through one of these minefields on their way back to Rossum.

Willem instructed his family on how to safely get through the field. "I will take the lead and carry the dog," he told them. "Geert, you will follow me and place your feet in my exact footprints. Kees, Sussie and Gerard, you will in turn follow each other behind your mother and walk only in the footprints of the one in front of you, and leave some distance between you, just in case. In this way, we can all go safely through the minefield."

Sussie was really scared. She knew what a mine could do to the person who stepped on it. She had heard about that during the war. The Cretier family carefully crossed the dangerous field looking like a father and mother duck with all their ducklings following along behind.

After they made it safely to the other side, they stopped for a moment to consider their accomplishment. They had done the seemingly impossible twice now as a family. They had escaped from the Germans while under fire a few months earlier and now they had safely crossed a minefield to return home unscathed. This was nothing short of a miracle!

When they reached the town of Rossum, their joy quickly turned to sorrow. They were disappointed to see that Rossum had fallen into a state of disrepair. Grass and weeds covered the streets and sidewalks. Most of the buildings were either damaged from grenades and shells or had been completely demolished. The sight was depressing.

As they approached their house, they noticed that the windows were boarded up. This did not look like a good sign. When they entered the home that had meant so much to them, they could only stop and stare. Everything that they had left behind was now gone except for Sussie's bed. Her cute little bed with the pretty white bedspread was covered in human excrement and urine. The Nazis had used her bedroom for a toilet.

'How could anyone do such a despicable act of destruction?' the Cretiers asked themselves. The sight before them was beyond their comprehension.

There were some badly painted pictures of German scenery on the walls that didn't belong there and the windows all had the glass busted out of them. At least someone had thought to board up the broken windows to keep out the weather. The entire house smelled terrible and was unfit for human habitation. While they stood there taking in this scene of devastation, Geert's mother arrived.

"I know this looks really bad and I feel your pain," she said, giving her daughter a big hug, "but we can start again. First, we will clean the house from top to bottom. Then we will fix your windows. I have saved all kinds of things for you – just about everything you need to live in your house again. In the meantime, you will have to come and stay with us until we make this place liveable again."

Dear sweet Oma. She had been hiding everything she could find, just waiting for the day her daughter and family were able to come home. The Germans had considered Sussie's grandparents too old to travel and had allowed them to stay in the German-occupied zone after the forced evacuation in February.

The Cretiers heard that after they had escaped, most of the other people of Rossum and surrounding area had been sent 50 kilometres north to Friesland. Many of them died of hunger. Once again, the Cretiers considered themselves lucky.

For the next few days, Geert and her family stayed with her parents while everyone pitched in to clean their house. Willem returned to Tilburg to give a week's notice at his job and then work for that week.

Opa had converted the brick kiln into a huge bedroom where many of Sussie's uncles, aunts and cousins had sought safe refuge from the conflict being fought outside. Now that the war was over, every family member could start to rebuild their lives.

Everyone was happy to see Sussie, Kees and Gerard. There were hugs and tears from Sussie's aunts and many remarks were made on how much the children had all grown in the eight months since their escape. Sussie's uncles were excited when they heard that she had saved quite a hoard of cigarettes that the Canadian soldiers had given her. She also had some large tins full of cookies she had saved for coming home. Soon, all Sussie's relatives were begging her for cigarettes and cookies. Sussie felt very important sharing her carefully saved goods with her extended family.

A week of cleaning, scrubbing and repairs to the Cretier home returned it to a decent condition again. Willem returned from Tilburg on the motorcycle, happy that he had been allowed to keep the bike. Then he opened the door to his workshop. Everything he had left in the shop months earlier was now gone. All his mechanic's tools, car parts, tires and everything else. The Germans had left nothing.

Willem then remembered storing some items in the garage attic for Ben Salet, a friend who was a well-known maker of fine furniture. Ben had been afraid the Germans would take all the stock from his shop and had asked Willem to hide what he could in the little space above the parts storage area. Willem opened the trap door to the attic.

"Geert!" he called, "come and look at this!"

Geert walked over from the house to see what was making Willem so excited.

"All Ben's furniture that we hid up here is still here! I guess the Germans didn't think there would be anything of value up there," Willem exclaimed. "I'm going to tell Ben right now. He will be one happy man to know he has enough stock to start his business again!"

Willem was correct and Ben soon re-opened his business and became very successful. As a gesture of thanks, he gave Geert and Willem a good deal on a new bedroom suite and a beautifully crafted table and chairs. Those pieces of exquisite handmade furniture stayed in the Cretier family from that day forward.

* * * * *

For Sussie and her brothers, adjusting to being home again was a little more difficult than they had imagined. Many of the areas where they used to play were now declared out of bounds because of the landmines still buried in the ground. Every once in awhile, there was a sad reminder of the dangers still lurking in their midst. Three boys from Sussie's school class were playing by the riverbank one day when they triggered one of these deadly devices. Two of the boys were killed instantly and the other sustained irreparable injuries, leaving him with permanent physical and mental disabilities.

One pleasant evening, a Jewish family returning from years in hiding stopped to ask directions to Heerewaarden. "Don't go over the bridge by the lock or near the dykes," the locals warned. "They haven't been cleared of mines yet."

The family had been hiding from the Nazis for more than four years and they wanted their peaceful life back. They were desperate to return to their home and they decided to take their chances. They ignored the warnings and drove their large truck toward the lock. Minutes later, the townspeople heard a loud explosion near the bridge.

"Oh, my God!" Willem exclaimed when he heard the bang. "They will all be dead!"

Willem and some other men raced to the bridge to see if they could help. The police were already there, keeping everyone away from the accident. The truck was destroyed. Only two members of the family survived. Both were badly injured.

"The Germans are gone, but will the war ever be really over for us?" Willem reflected as the whole town of Rossum mourned the needless loss of these good people.

Gradually, the mines were cleared away and more and more people were able to safely return to their homes.

Although repairing their house was the first priority for the Cretiers, the whole community was involved in rebuilding. The school, churches, town hall and many other buildings needed attention. Slowly, these industrious people worked together to put their lives back in order.

During that first summer back in Rossum, Sussie made friends with the de Leeuw family who owned a dairy farm nearby. They had two sons and a daughter. One afternoon they asked Sussie, "Would you like come help us milk the cows?"

Sussie never had to be asked twice to try something new and she quickly agreed. 'How hard can it be to milk a cow?' she thought to herself.

Jan, one of the brothers, gave Sussie a little stool and showed her how to sit beside the cow and spray the milk into a pail. Sussie soon learned that this seemingly simple task was not as easy as it looked. She sprayed milk on herself, was almost as nervous as the fidgety cow, couldn't believe how much her hands ached, and ended up getting very little milk in the pail. Finally, Jan offered to finish the job for Sussie.

Despite her inability to milk the cow on her first try, Sussie was determined to learn. "Can I come over and help every day?" she asked.

"You sure can," was the reply, "and you can ride one of the horses while we round up the cows for milking, too." So at 4:00 p.m. every day that summer, Sussie headed for the farm.

There were two horses on the dairy farm and Sussie was allowed to ride the old, quiet horse that walked everywhere at the same leisurely pace. He was a big horse and Sussie had to be helped up to sit on his back. It was a great way for a young girl to pass the summer.

Sussie's mother, however, didn't find it quite as entertaining. "You smell like a farm," Geert told Sussie one day. "Pretty soon the house will smell like a farm, too."

When summer ended, so did Sussie's visits to the dairy farm.

Life for the Cretiers soon became as normal as could be expected after such a long ordeal. Sussie was happy that she had something very special to remind her of the soldiers who had restored their freedom. There were many times when she took her little coat out of the closet, set it on her bed and looked at it lovingly.

The little coat was her reality check, a reminder of the sacrifice that some young men from a far-away land had made for her country.

These Canadian soldiers would always be her heroes and the little coat was a part of them that she would hold dear forever.

CHAPTER TWELVE

Back to the Netherlands

When Bob arrived in Paisley after the war, he was greeted with a royal homecoming. Uncle Archie and Auntie Nan showered him with affection, and put on some great parties with every one of Bob's Scottish relatives in attendance.

War effort programs were still in effect with food being rationed, so Bob thought he would help out his aunt and uncle. After all, he was enjoying their hospitality for free.

"Auntie Nan, take my ration book to buy extra food," Bob offered.

"No, Bob," his aunt replied. "You take your ration book down to the store in your nice Canadian Army uniform and smile nicely at the storekeeper. I know she will give you a lot more than she would give me."

The female storekeeper not only proved Auntie Nan right, she asked Bob for a date, too! This was not uncommon behaviour for a Scottish girl when a good-looking Canadian soldier presented himself. Bob politely refused her request.

One morning, when Uncle Archie was leaving for work, he invited Bob to join him at a local pub at the end of his work day. "We can have a wee dram on the way home," Archie suggested.

"Okay," Bob answered. "I'll be there."

So Bob waited for his uncle at the gates of the mill at 5:00 p.m. when all 5,000 female employees of the mill came through the gate. At least 100 of those women propositioned

Bob. He was red-faced by the attention and politely refused all of them. Behind the last of the girls leaving the factory was Uncle Archie, highly amused at Bob's obvious embarrassment. Bob suffered considerable ribbing from his uncle on the way home that evening and from his uncle's friends at the pubs they visited.

Being back in Scotland with these favourite relatives was a wonderful time for Bob after all he had experienced. It still felt a bit strange to know that the fighting was over. He was a soldier after all, trained to fight wars. It was going to take him awhile to get used to civilian life.

Bob's 10 days of bliss in Scotland came to an end too quickly and he had to return to his regiment. By then, the troops were gathered in the Netherlands, so Bob joined them there.

The Dutch were celebrating their freedom in a big way. Every town and city in the Netherlands had arranged its own Victory parade and the Canadian soldiers were amazed at the amount of liquor that appeared for these celebrations.

When the soldiers asked where all the liquor came from, the locals told them, "Nix in de winkel, alses in de kelder." Nothing in the stores. Everything in the cellar.

The Canadians had quite a chuckle over that phrase.

Bob missed many of the informal Victory celebrations when he was on leave in Scotland, but he was back in time for the formal Victory parades. The first one involving the Canadian military was on May 21 at The Hague. There was another on June 6 in Utrecht and one in Amsterdam on June 28. Bob had accumulated many cigarettes over the previous month and during these parades, he was able to give away thousands of cigarettes to the Dutch people who were climbing onto the tanks to kiss, hug and shake the hands of their heroes.

When the final parade in Amsterdam ended, the cook wagon came by to distribute meals to all the soldiers. Still basking in the glow of the Dutch people's gratitude, the soldiers grabbed their mess cans and cups and collected their rations from the wagon. The food on this day seemed abnormally good. The mashed potatoes were always appreciated and there were green beans and a piece of chicken for each of them.

'Well, they said it was chicken and it looks like chicken, but it doesn't exactly taste like chicken,' Bob thought to himself. Still, it was about as good a meal as one could expect from a cook wagon making enough meals for a thousand men.

As Bob's crew went to empty their leftovers into the barrels provided for that purpose, a little Dutch boy was waiting for them. He indicated that he wanted them to put their scraps into the pail he was holding.

"Voor de swine," he told them. For the pigs.

The troops obliged, but a few minutes later, Bob peered around the corner to see where the little boy had gone. There he was, eating the leftovers out of the pail, including tea leaves that had been emptied from the soldiers' cups.

Bob's compassion coursed through him as strong as it ever had. He took the boy by the hand, led him to the cook wagon and got him a fresh meal to eat. Bob sat with the boy while the youngster slowly ate every morsel on the plate. Judging his age at about six years old, Bob decided that the poor little boy had probably not had a decent meal for most of his life. After he had eaten his fill, the boy was so grateful that he washed all the dirty dishes in the cook wagon.

'I feel so sorry for these kids,' Bob thought to himself later that day. 'Their war is not over yet. Their fight against hunger and malnutrition is still going on. I wish I could do more for them.'

With the Victory parades behind them, the soldiers had no further use for their armaments. They spent the next few days cleaning and painting their tanks, trucks and equipment. Then they had parade ground drill and the final regimental parade. After that, Bob and his crew said goodbye to the tank that had been their virtual home for so long. It was ready to be shipped back to Canada along with the rest of the military equipment.

The soldiers who remained from the 19th Field Regiment were assigned to Zeist, a small town outside of Utrecht in southern Netherlands, where they were supposed to provide security and assist the Dutch with their reconstruction. Bob was assigned to the post of quartermaster sergeant there, responsible for the Army's store and warehouse in the area.

Walking through the huge pile of provisions in the warehouse one day, Bob thought about the Dutch people outside those warehouse doors. 'We've got plenty of food here. More than we'll ever use,' he said to himself.

His thoughts quickly turned to action and he loaded a large truck with as much food as it would carry, then drove into Amsterdam and gave all the supplies away. Bob felt a lot better after that. He had done something positive for the children who had suffered so much at the hands of the Nazis.

He repeated this trip as many times as he could while there were supplies to be shared. He reasoned that it wasn't right that little children should suffer and it wasn't wrong for him to give them what was plentiful in the Army stores.

No one in the Canadian Army questioned Bob's generosity with their wares. Many other quartermasters in other affected regions may have done similar good deeds. For Bob and these others, it was simply the right thing to do.

Meanwhile, thousands upon thousands of German prisoners of war were being sent back to Germany. There were seemingly endless columns of them marching by on the streets of the Netherlands, with a very minimal Allied guard overseeing their passage. Bob was watching this long line of German soldiers one day when he noticed that a lot of the prisoners had Dutch bicycles with them and were carrying as many looted goods as they could. This was Bob's cue to intervene.

"Hey, you!" he yelled at some of the prisoners. "You get off those bikes and you drop everything you have but the things you came here with!"

Bob was so annoyed by the audacity of these remnants of the German Army, trying to steal from the already poverty-stricken Dutch people. He didn't care whether they understood English or not. With his yelling and motions, Bob made sure that these prisoners received his message that they were not going to be taking anything that didn't belong to them back to Germany. Until the last of those German POWs left the Netherlands, Bob made it his mission to alternate his time between feeding the Dutch people and relieving the greedy German soldiers of their ill-gotten gains.

Bob discovered other oddities during these post-war months. Cigarettes were still good currency and when he had his hair trimmed at a shop in The Hague one day, he was told that his payment for the haircut was, "Four cigarettes, please."

On another occasion, Bob was with a group of fellow soldiers in a café in Rotterdam. A well-dressed man approached their table and asked if he could clean out their ashtray. "Sure," Bob replied, "go ahead."

The man emptied the contents of the ashtray into a little bag and left. "Who was that?" Bob asked the waiter after the gentleman had gone.

"He is an official from the town hall," the waiter answered.

"So, why would he want the cigarette butts?"

"He will make them into more cigarettes," said the waiter.

"Boy, I hope I'm never that broke," Bob murmured.

On one of their free evenings, the Canadians visited a nightclub in Utrecht called De Raadskelder. They were surprised to find that the house band playing there was a group of talented black musicians from the United States. These men had been playing in the club when the Nazis took control in 1940 and had not been able to go home since then.

"We've been stuck here for five years," the band leader told Bob one night, "and every winter I've nearly frozen to death. You wouldn't happen to have some spare winter underwear we could have, would you?"

"Sure," Bob replied. "I think I can accommodate you with that one." The next time Bob and his buddies went to De Raadskelder, they took two sets of winter underwear for each member of the band.

"Hey, this is great. Thanks a whole bunch," the band leader said. "What's your favourite song?"

"Home On The Range," Bob replied, thinking of the great Canadian Prairies he hadn't seen in a long time.

"You got it," the band leader said, and they proceeded to play the song beautifully. Every time Bob entered the club after that, the band stopped whatever song they were playing and launched into 'Home On The Range' in Bob's honour. Those extra pairs of underwear had gone a long way to make the De Raadskelder club Bob's new home away from home for the remainder of his stay in the Netherlands.

One day when he was at the Army store, Bob received a list naming all the surplus food and clothing that was to be boxed up and sent back to Canada. The list said he should send 25 pairs of leather boots. Bob counted 500 pairs in the store and decided that all those Dutch men wearing wooden clogs would probably rather be wearing leather boots. The rest of the list of items to be sent home was similar in nature, requiring only about a third of what was in stock to be sent back to Canada. When Bob asked what he should do with the remainder of the items, he was told, "Just get rid of it."

Bob gladly obliged.

Although he wanted to give away the extra items to the Dutch people, they would not accept these items as gifts. They insisted on paying something for the goods and Bob ended up with a wheelbarrow full of Dutch guilders, which bought plenty of watery beer for the Army boys when they visited De Raadskelder. The Canadian soldiers were only allowed to each take 600 guilders out of the country, so they had to do something with the rest of their profit. Bob later thought that he should have bought some property with his share of the money but, being young, he just blew it all and went home happy.

* * * * *

Near the middle of June, before he went back to Canada, Bob started thinking about his upcoming birthday. On June 26, he would be 20 years old – very young for a soldier with four years of military service. He knew exactly how he wanted to celebrate his special birthday and he sought out two of his old tank crew to help him.

"George! Duke! My birthday is coming up and I was thinking that maybe we should head up to Rossum and visit with the Cretiers," he told them.

"I'll be in on that one," Duke quickly replied.

"Me, too," said George. "Sounds like a great idea."

There were Canadian Army trucks running back and forth all over the Netherlands at the time, so it was easy for these three comrades-in-arms to hitch a ride wherever they wanted to go. The last truck they rode in dropped them off about five miles from their destination, so they had to use the Army Boot Express for the rest of the way into Rossum.

The trio of travelers was almost at the town, walking along the top of the dyke, when they spotted Sussie. She was carrying an armful of shoebox mines! Bob nearly had a heart attack when she suddenly dropped the whole bundle on the ground and came running up the dyke toward them shouting, "Bob, Bob, Bob!"

(Later, Bob learned that the shoebox mines had all been defused and emptied of their lethal contents. The children were using them for toys.)

Sussie was so happy to see her favourite soldiers again! She quickly gave them all a big hug. "I still have the coat you gave me," she immediately told them. "I'll keep it for the rest of my life!"

"That's great, Sussie," said Bob, looking around at their surroundings. "It's a good thing we met you here. Now you can show us the way to your house."

"Oh, I can do that all right," Sussie continued. "This is so good! I didn't think I would ever see you guys again."

Sussie talked as they walked, telling the men about the day her family had to walk through the minefields to get home and what their house looked like when they got there. She was so excited to be with her heroes again.

"Mom! Dad!" Sussie called as she came through their doorway. "Look who I found wandering along the dyke!"

Willem and Geert were overwhelmed to see these three fine young soldiers who had treated them so well during the war. "Come in, come in," Willem said. "And what brings you here on this fine day?"

"It's Bob's birthday," Duke blurted out.

George finished his sentence, "And he figured he would like to spend it with the best friends we have in all of the Netherlands!"

This was a marvellous reunion for the men and Willem, Geert and their three children. Geert cooked a wonderful supper while Willem showed his Canadian Army buddies his reopened workshop.

"There's not much here yet," he explained as he gave them the grand tour. "The Germans took everything, but I will rise again." Then they all went back into the house to enjoy Geert's home-cooked meal.

After supper, Willem suggested, "I think we should take our friends to the bar to celebrate Bob's birthday."

"I think so, too," Geert agreed.

"Can I come, too?" Sussie asked. "Please, please let me come, too."

"No," Willem answered, "You are too young to go there. I want you three to go to bed when we go out."

'This is not fair!' Sussie thought, feeling very unhappy. 'These are my soldiers! I should be allowed to be with them.'

Willem and Geert ignored their pouting daughter and left for the bar with Bob, George and Duke to celebrate Bob's birthday. The three Canadians hardly paid for a drink all night. The people of Rossum showed their appreciation to these men who were their heroes. They had plenty to talk about, too, with all the incidents that had happened to both the soldiers and the Cretiers since the Canadians left to fight their final battles.

The next morning, Bob and his two crewmen said a heartfelt goodbye to their good friends, the Cretiers, after promising to keep in touch. The men hitchhiked their way back to Zeist, catching rides all the way back to their unit.

A while later, another memo was delivered to Bob at the Army store. The Canadian government had donated some trucks to Czechoslovakia and Bob was to arrange for their delivery. He thought about the logistics of the process and decided he would like to be one of the drivers to take the trucks to Czechoslovakia.

Bob was not prepared for the devastation he saw on that journey, however. Every city and town in every country they drove through had experienced extensive damage to its buildings. The roads and bridges didn't fare too well either, causing the convoy to make several detours.

"It's going to be a long time before these poor people have anything that resembles a normal life," Bob commented to George when they stopped for food and refuelling at one point.

"That's for sure," George said. "We are the lucky ones. We get to go home to our country that didn't get a scratch out of all this."

Upon his return to Zeist from Czechoslovakia, Bob was transferred back to his original 13th Regiment. The Calgary-based unit would travel home together.

Bob's remaining days in the Netherlands were spent playing soccer, going to De Raadskelder and just generally wasting time. In November 1945, his regiment was returned to Aldershot Barracks in the south of England, retracing the path that he had taken to go into war.

At Aldershot, Bob was placed in charge of the sergeants' mess. His luck was still holding. This position enabled him to hold some good parties and he was able to visit Scotland one more time to say goodbye to all his relatives before he was shipped home to Canada.

Finally, on the morning of February 2, 1946, Bob and another 22,000 Canadian soldiers boarded the RMS Queen Elizabeth for their voyage home. The trip across the Atlantic took four and a half days. This time there were no detours to extend their voyage and no German U-boats with deadly torpedoes waiting silently below the waves to send them to Davy Jones' Locker.

Above left: Bob Elliott at the end of the war, May 1945, with his Sexton SP 'tank.' Note the 'Evelyne' painted on the tank's body.
Above right: The starving Dutch boy who collected the Canadian soldiers' leftovers in his pail.

Above: German soldiers marching home after the war, Netherlands, 1945.

Below left: William Elliott Sr., Bob's father, in his Canadian Army uniform in Calgary, Alberta, Canada.
Below right: The buildings from left to right are the Cretiers' house, parts store and garage in Rossum, Netherlands.

CHAPTER THIRTEEN

Together forever

On February 6, 1946, the RMS Queen Elizabeth berthed in New York Harbour where all 22,000 of her live military cargo eagerly disembarked. Getting back on the North American continent after four, five or even six years of war was the realization of a long-sought-after dream for each of the soldiers.

Bob still had a long way to go to get back to his Canadian home in Calgary, though. The train trip from New York to Calgary, Alberta, took the same length of time as the Atlantic crossing. Another four and a half days.

On February 11, 1946, Bob's long and tiring journey came to an end. His father was at the train station to welcome him.

"It's great to have you home, Bob," William Elliott said as he shook his son's hand. "I am so thankful that all my sons made it back alive, in one piece. There are so many fathers who didn't have that privilege."

Bob's father had been in the Army as well, as a quartermaster sergeant with the reserves in Calgary. Bob was proud of his father for doing his bit for the war.

In Calgary, there was no big heroes' welcome or parade for Bob like there had been for the first group of soldiers who came home and then went to fight in the Pacific. By this time, most Canadians had forgotten about the war and were getting on with their lives.

"I've got some news for you," Bob's father said as they were driving home. "Your brother John got divorced and headed back to England. He must have passed you somewhere on the

Atlantic. He says he's going to marry some girl called Kathleen that he met over there. Did you meet her?"

"Yes, I did," Bob answered. "She's a really nice girl, Dad." Nothing more was said on that topic. As far as Bob was concerned, John was old enough to make his own decisions. The conversation did cause Bob to wonder whatever happened to the girls that he had dated here in Calgary before going to war, however. Some had sent him 'Dear John' letters while he was overseas, and there were others he thought he should check on to see about the possibilities of them getting together.

After a great supper and a warm welcome from his mother, Bob made some phone calls only to discover that all the girls he knew before he left Canada were either married or engaged. 'I guess that's what happens when you disappear for five years,' he thought.

"Will you be staying here or do you have to go to the barracks?" Robina Elliott asked her son after supper.

"I have 30 days leave before my discharge," Bob answered, "so, if you don't mind, I'd like to stay here. You're a better cook than they are."

"That's the only reason you want to stay here? My cooking?" his mother asked, slightly offended.

"Just kidding," Bob grinned. "Anyway, I want to visit with my brothers and sisters while I can, so I won't be around much."

Over the next few weeks, Bob spent time with all of his siblings except for his sister Betty and her husband Bob Morrison who had moved to British Columbia. Getting reacquainted with his brothers and sisters was an enjoyable experience. His sister Peggy and her husband Jack Stirton still farmed near Olds, Alberta, and while Bob was helping them pull stumps from their fields one day, he almost tore his thumb off.

Dr. Mann, the same physician in Olds who had sewn up Bob's shortened fingers when he was young, sewed up this injury as well, but Bob would never be able to bend his right thumb again after this accident.

"I think you'd better stay away from Olds," Dr. Mann advised while he tended to Bob's injured thumb. "You can live through the worst battles of the Second World War virtually unscathed, then the moment you come here, you get injured. I think the best medicine I can prescribe is to bar you from this town," the doctor said.

"Alright," Bob laughed. "I know when I'm not wanted. I promise I'll leave first thing in the morning."

On March 12, 1946, Bob headed back to Calgary to receive his official discharge from the Canadian Army. Now he would no longer receive a military paycheque, so he had to look for a job.

After a short stint working on a farm about 30 miles north of Calgary near Carstairs, Bob signed on as an apprentice electrician with Electrical Contracting Co. of Calgary for a starting wage of 44.5 cents an hour. He completed his apprenticeship and wrote and passed his final exam in 1948.

He was now a full-fledged electrician with aspirations of advancing in his field. While reading a local newspaper, he noticed an ad for an electrician with Otis Elevator Company for more money than his present hourly journeyman rate of $1.10, so he applied for the job. Bob was hired and spent the next six years working as an elevator mechanic.

The year 1948 was a busy one for Bob. He had met Grace Fleming at a dance in Calgary the previous year. She worked at a local bakery and they fell in love and were married in 1948. He also built their first house in 1948 and near the end of the year, he received the news that his father had been diagnosed with liver cancer. William Elliott stayed with Bob and his new wife in Calgary for awhile but then moved out to stay at his daughter Peggy's farm at Olds. Two months after that, his health deteriorated and he was hospitalized in Olds.

Bob spent many nights hitchhiking from Calgary to Olds to visit his father. William Elliott Senior died shortly afterwards and was given a funeral with military honours in Olds. This was a sad loss for Bob and his family. His father was only 59 years old. (Bob's mother Robina died in 1962 at age 73.)

* * * * *

In 1950, Bob's youngest brother Charles (Chuck) signed up for Army duty and went to Germany as an occupational soldier. This completed the military history of the Elliott family. The father and all his five of his sons had served their country in the Canadian Armed Forces.

In 1954, the manager at Otis Elevator recognized Bob's leadership qualities and offered him the job of superintendent at their Edmonton branch office. He came to the site where Bob was working to present this job offer and he didn't give Bob much of a chance to turn him down.

"I suppose you'd like to talk it over with your wife," the manager asked after he'd offered Bob the job.

"Sure, I would," Bob replied.

"Good," said the manager. "Come with me. I'll drive you home and wait in the car for you. We need an answer right now."

Bob's wife agreed to the transfer, which meant a substantial pay raise for Bob, and they moved to Edmonton. Bob enjoyed a long career with Otis, working as superintendent and then Edmonton district manager, then transferring to Hamilton, Ontario, to become manager of field operations there. In his last role with the company, he was personnel manager of benefits and field operations. It was a challenging position and he thoroughly enjoyed it.

During these years, Bob and his wife raised three children. Sharon was born in 1949, Heather in 1952 and Mark in 1954. They later adopted another daughter, Theresa, born in 1962.

Through it all, Bob kept his promise of keeping in touch with his wartime friends in the Netherlands. The Elliotts and Cretiers exchanged Christmas cards and letters over all those years. On numerous occasions, Bob invited his friend Willem Cretier to go hunting near Nordegg, northwest of Olds, Alberta, where Bob's one brother was a Forestry Service ranger. The Cretiers were never able to come to Canada, though, so that hunting trip never materialized.

* * * * *

At the beginning of February 1981, Bob received an invitation from Willem and Geert Cretier to attend their 50th wedding anniversary celebration. It was to be held on February 19 in Rossum. Bob had recently separated from his wife after 32 years of marriage and he had already made arrangements to travel to Scotland later that spring to visit his Uncle Archie and Auntie Nan. Although he couldn't attend the Cretiers' anniversary celebration, he thought he would just pop over to the Netherlands and visit his Dutch friends in May instead of in February, saving the cost of two trips to Europe.

A few months later, Bob spent a wonderful two weeks visiting his uncle and aunt. His aunt recognized, though, that Bob was lonely. She knew he was looking forward to seeing his friends the Cretiers again and she had a funny feeling about Bob's future. As he was leaving Scotland, Auntie Nan gave Bob a hug and wished him well.

"Well, son, I hope you find what you're looking for," she told him.

* * * * *

In Rossum after the war, Willem and Geert Cretier set about rebuilding their lives and their business. There was also a new addition to their family. On January 22, 1947, another son was born. He was named after his father. Willem Jan brought much joy to his parents and siblings, filling them with laughter as they watched him explore his surroundings and take his first steps.

During this time, there was a renewed sense of hope in the future of the Netherlands. Queen Wilhelmina was home again and had a new granddaughter who had been born in Canada to her daughter Princess Juliana. The queen, by her speeches of encouragement over the BBC during the war, had endeared herself to the people. She wasn't just loved. She was revered. The resilience of the Dutch people in rebuilding their country was truly remarkable, with a swift return to a stable economy. No other country rebuilt its economy as quickly as the resourceful people of the Netherlands.

Sussie Cretier grew into a sweet young woman. She finished high school and become a teacher of handicrafts and embroidery. At age 20, she married Frans van Leeuwen and helped him with his taxi and tour bus business. In 1960, their first child was born. Trudy brought a new joy to Sussie's life. Three years later, their son Harold was born. The happiness of this event was short-lived.

Harold was born with a rare blood disorder known as the Rhesus Factor. He lived for only three days. Sussie was devastated. The emptiness she felt was indescribable. As always, her mother was there to help her through this crisis, looking after Trudy and comforting Sussie in her grief. From that day forward, Sussie carried the memory of her little Harold with her in her heart.

Two years later, another son was born. This time, the doctors were aware of the possibility of Rhesus Factor and took the necessary steps to avoid another crisis. Five-year-old Trudy was so happy with her baby brother Erwin that she brought the little pram that her grandmother had given her to the hospital to take the baby home.

While Sussie cared for her young children, she was also busy with another challenging job. Her ability to manage complicated tasks had landed her a position as general manager of Family Welcome for all of the Netherlands. Two years later, she required a hysterectomy and had to resign from her job to recuperate at home. She became a stay-at-home mom, but her marriage faltered and she and her husband separated.

True to her resilient character, Sussie did not take long to find employment again. She worked in a restaurant in Switzerland for awhile and then moved back to Rossum to work as a night shift attendant at a senior citizens' home. She thoroughly enjoyed this position and spent many hours talking about the past with the residents there.

On May 12, 1981, Sussie was at home talking with her children when her telephone rang. She answered and a voice from the past spoke to her.

"Hi. Bob Elliott here."

"Oh, hi, Bob. It's nice to hear from you. How have you been?"

It didn't seem to matter that they hadn't spoken to each other in 36 years. They just picked up right where they had left off decades earlier.

"Fine, fine. I'm coming to Holland tomorrow."

"That's nice, Bob. Where are you landing and what time do you get here?"

"I'll be on a KLM flight from Glasgow with a stop in Aberdeen and then to Amsterdam, arriving at 7:45 a.m."

"Okay, do you need someone to pick you up?" Sussie asked.

"No, that's okay. I have to go to the bank to change some money when I get there, then I'll rent a car."

"Okay, I'll see you tomorrow," Sussie said and then hung up.

After a few moments, the significance of the phone call sank in for Sussie.

'Oh my goodness!' she thought. 'This is my soldier coming to see us! My hero, and the one who gave me my fabulous little coat! I'd better make sure someone is there to meet him. We were all there to meet him and his fellow soldiers in 1944 and we should be there now.'

Sussie phoned her parents to tell them the news. She asked if they could go pick up Bob from the airport, but Willem was ill and unable to go, so Sussie phoned her brothers. Kees was sick, too, and Gerard could barely remember Bob. Willem Jr. hadn't even been born when Bob was in the Netherlands, so he wasn't the right one to send either. So Sussie resolved to go to the airport herself, even if it meant getting no sleep after work that night.

The next morning, Sussie went home after her night shift, changed her clothes and immediately drove the 90 minutes to Amsterdam to meet Bob. At the airport, she watched the monitor screens for news of Bob's flight. Nothing was posted indicating whether the flight had arrived or not.

'I wonder if he's here already,' she thought. 'Maybe I'm late.' Then other thoughts crowded her mind. 'What if I don't recognize him? It's been 36 years since I saw him last. I'm sure he's changed.'

So Sussie found a piece of plain paper and wrote 'ELLIOTT' on it in big bold letters. Holding up this notice, she wandered around the airport in the hope that Bob would spot her.

Then she remembered what Bob had said about going to the bank and renting a car. 'I'll go look in the bank,' she thought.

The Amsterdam airport had been busy that morning with line-ups at every counter, and the bank was no different. As Sussie approached the line of people patiently waiting their turn, she noticed a man whom she thought looked familiar from the back. He looked a little heavier than she remembered him being, but she was sure it was Bob, so she walked up behind him and tapped him on the shoulder.

"Are you Bob?" she asked.

The man turned around and smiled. "Sussie!" he yelled.

This was definitely Bob Elliott! He gave Sussie a hug that nearly took all the wind out of her. Then he lifted her off the floor and spun her around before letting her down again.

"You didn't have to come for me, but I sure appreciate the welcome," he said. "It's great to see you again and you look great, too!"

"You look pretty good yourself, Bob," Sussie said.

After Bob finished his business at the bank, they made their way out of the airport. While they were walking to the car and chatting, Sussie surprised herself by thinking, 'If I'm not careful, I could fall in love with this man. Goodness me, what am I thinking? I haven't seen him in over three decades and already he has an effect on me! And I vowed I would never fall in love again!'

The trip back to Rossum was filled with memories and small talk. Again, Sussie's thoughts surprised her. 'It wouldn't be right for him to stay with me at my house,' she said to herself.

Then she said aloud, "You should stay at Mom and Dad's house. There would be a lot of gossip if you stayed with me. You know, 'A strange man in her house,' etc."

"That's fine with me," Bob said. "I am looking forward to spending some time with my old friend Willem."

Seeing Willem and Geert after all those years was very emotional for Bob and the Cretiers. Many hugs, kisses, handshakes and tears were shared in those first few moments. Once they settled down for a visit, Geert whispered in her daughter's ear, "Go and get your little coat. I bet Bob will be surprised to see that you still have it."

So Sussie went to her mother's closet where her prized possession had been stored for many years. Sussie carefully took her little coat off its hanger and carried it out to the living room.

Bob could not believe his eyes. "Holy mackerel!" he exclaimed. "You still have that, after all these years?"

While Bob seemed pleased, Sussie wasn't quite sure. Her understanding of the English language had diminished somewhat over the years and she had to ask for an explanation.

"What is a mackerel?" she asked innocently.

Bob burst into laughter. "It's a fish. But that's just a saying we use in Canada when we are surprised by something. And I am really surprised to see that you kept that little coat all this time."

"This little coat means more to me than anything I have in the world, except for my children," Sussie told him. "It is my connection to you and all the other soldiers who gave it to me. Every time I look at it, I get the same wonderful feeling I had on the day you gave it to me. I will never, ever forget the happiness you gave to me on that cold Christmas morning, and it is still the most beautiful piece of clothing I own."

Bob was completely humbled by Sussie's display of appreciation. He marvelled at the good condition in which the Cretiers had preserved her little coat. All the brass buttons that he and the other crew members had taken off their own tunics were still intact and the coat didn't look any different than the day it was given to her.

Soon, Sussie excused herself from the happy reunion so she could go home to bed after her sleepless night and exciting day. She would only get a few hours sleep before starting her night shift again. Willem, Geert and Bob enjoyed a great supper together and visited for a few more hours, rekindling their friendship as if it had never lapsed.

The next morning, Willem said to Geert, "I don't think Bob is very happy. I heard him pacing the floor all last night."

"He probably still has nightmares from the war," Geert replied, knowing that many soldiers suffered for years after the battles had ended. Out of courtesy, neither of them mentioned their observations to Bob.

The Cretiers and Bob spent the next couple of days reminiscing about their wartime experiences and talking about their families, filling in all the gaps between the past 35 Christmases.

"Sussie is getting divorced and she lives by herself now," Willem told Bob one day.

"I didn't know that," Bob replied. "I separated from my wife as well. It's a real shame. Everything was going well for many years – at least you think it was – and then all of a sudden, everything changed and you wonder where it all went wrong."

Nothing more was said about marital status for awhile.

During the few days he had in the Netherlands, Bob wanted to see some of the other families he had known during the war, so Sussie offered to drive him wherever he wanted to go. These families welcomed Bob with open arms. They were surprised to see him and took him into their homes as though he was a royal guest. He had saved their country, or at least helped immensely to get them to freedom.

Bob continued to deny that he was a hero. He was only doing his job, he told them. But that's not how the Dutch people saw it. They still loved him and his countrymen, many decades later.

As Bob and Sussie drove around to the homes in Rossum and area, they talked about their lives and their families. The more they talked, the more they realized how much they had in common. Soon, Sussie found herself thinking, 'I can feel us getting closer and closer. This man is my hero. He was the one who always made me feel safe and important during the war, and he still does!'

"Mom tells me you are not married anymore," Sussie said to Bob one day as they were driving.

"No, we're separated," Bob replied casually, "I'll be starting divorce proceedings when I get home."

Nothing was said for a few more moments. Then Sussie spoke. "Life can be very difficult at times, hey, Bob?"

"Yeah," Bob answered quietly. After a short pause, he added, "It sure can."

Both Sussie and Bob could feel their bond grow stronger with each minute they spent together.

Over the next couple of days, Willem noticed the special looks that his daughter had for Bob, not to mention the increasing amount of time they were spending together, Sussie's growing happiness, and the twinkle in Bob's eyes when he and Sussie were together. Willem mentioned his observations to Geert.

"I think you'd better make the most of your time with Sussie. I have a feeling she will go to Canada with Bob."

"No, I don't think so," Geert said with conviction. "She has her family here. I think you are dreaming."

But Willem was about to be proven right.

Near the end of his five days in Rossum, while Bob and Sussie were taking in the sights and visiting with some of the other Dutch families, Bob flippantly asked Sussie, "Do you think you could live in Canada?"

"Oh, I don't know, Bob. I'll have to think about that one," Sussie replied. "I have my children here and my job."

Although her immediate reaction was to think of her family and her desire to stay close to them, Bob's question started the wheels of thought turning in Sussie's head. 'If I go, I will miss my kids. It's so far away. But if I stay here, I might miss out on a wonderful life with my favourite soldier. He was my hero when I was a child and I still love being with him.'

Neither of them gave any thought to their nine-year age difference. It didn't seem important. Their feelings for each other, which had just flooded out the moment they reconnected, took top priority.

"Okay, I'll go," Sussie said after another moment in thought, "but I'll need to keep in touch with my children."

"Permission unconditionally granted!" Bob stated in his best sober military tone.

On the inside, though, he was overjoyed that she had said, 'Yes.'

So Willem's prediction was realized and Sussie visited Bob in Canada twice during the next four months. On September 12, 1981, Bob flew to the Netherlands to permanently move Sussie to Canada. This was exactly four months to the day that

Bob called Sussie to announce his visit to Rossum. Now, she was ready to leave the Netherlands and follow her soldier to Canada.

One of the last items she packed in her luggage was her childhood Army coat. "I love this little coat and I'm taking it to Canada," she told Bob as she carefully placed her much-loved gift in a suitcase.

To be Dutch is to own a bicycle and Sussie was no exception to that rule, so one of the other important possessions that had to be transported to Canada was Sussie's bike.

Some of Sussie's friends were nervous about her moving to Canada. Her girlfriend Audrey Strueak came with Sussie on her first journey, to check Bob out and make sure Sussie would be comfortable in her new home. Audrey decided that Bob was obviously going to take good care of her friend, and she gave her blessing to their relationship before heading back to the Netherlands.

By 1981, Sussie's children were grown up and living on their own. Trudy was married and Erwin was studying at university. After Sussie moved to Canada, she missed her children immensely but she frequently talked to them by telephone and that made it feel as though they weren't so far away after all.

On the evening of Christmas Day that same year, word came from the Netherlands that Sussie's father Willem was very ill. To Sussie's surprise, Bob immediately took her to the airport and sent her back to Rossum to be with her father. She realized again in that moment what a caring and compassionate man Bob was, and she was again thankful for her decision to follow him to Canada. Sussie was even more grateful that she was able to be with Willem, holding his hand when he died on December 29.

Shortly after the funeral was over, Geert decided to send Sussie back to Canada, where she would be comforted by Bob. "You'd better get back to Bob. He needs you and you should be with him," Geert said. "Your father is gone now and we will miss him, but life must go on." Sussie took her mother's advice and flew back to Canada.

On February 23, 1985, Bob Elliott and Sussie Cretier were married in Hamilton, Ontario. They had a private ceremony with only two witnesses. That evening, they celebrated with a small group of close friends.

On that day, Sussie Cretier officially became Sue Elliott.

It seemed that the magic of the little coat had endured the passage of time and she was now married to the very soldier she had admired so long ago – her hero, her protector and now, her husband. Sue's heart was filled with joy as she began her new life in Canada.

And Bob finally had his little beacon of hope by his side, forever.

* * * * *

One evening not too long after they were married, Sue began thinking about Duke and wondered if he lived anywhere near them. "Have you ever seen Duke since the war?" she asked Bob.

"I haven't seen him in a long time, but I think he still lives here in Hamilton. I'll see if I can find him in the phone book."

It was not an easy task to find his friend Ernie Dawson in the telephone directory. There were literally dozens of Dawsons listed. Bob narrowed his search down to a few possible 'E. Dawsons,' picked one he thought would be most likely to be his old gun-loader buddy and dialed the number.

"Hello," a voice on the other end of the line said.

"Hi. Is this Ernie Dawson, the one that was known as Duke during the war?" Bob asked.

"Yes it is," came the reply. "So who wants to know?"

"This is Bob Elliott and I have someone with me that would like to talk to you."

"Oh, hi, Bob! And who would that be?" Duke asked.

"You figure it out," Bob said and handed the phone to Sue.

"Hi, Duke, how are you?" she asked.

"I'm just fine, but who are you?"

"This is Sussie."

The phone went silent for a few moments.

"Little Sussie from Holland?" Duke asked incredulously.

"Yes, it's me," Sue said.

Then Duke got excited. "You and Bob have got to come over right now!" he said. "Get a pen and write down our address!"

About an hour later, Bob and Sue stopped in front of Duke's house where he and his wife Clara had been standing at the window, watching for them. It was a great reunion, with Clara listening to all the stories as they reminisced of their days together in the Netherlands.

"You're not going to believe this," Bob said. "Sussie still has that little coat we made for her in 1944."

"Really? No way!" Duke exclaimed. "You kept it all this time? That's incredible!"

So Bob and Sue and Duke told Clara about the coat. They shared some of their other adventures and had a wonderful visit. This meeting and the memories of the little coat renewed their friendship and they promised to keep in touch from then on.

In 1987, Bob retired from his job with Otis Elevators in Hamilton. With nothing to keep him in Ontario any longer, he and Sue moved to Edmonton, Alberta, to be near Bob's daughter Sharon Melnyk. Later that year, Sue heard from her family in the Netherlands that her mother Geert had been diagnosed with Alzheimer's disease and was in a nursing home.

"I would really like to be near my mother," Sue told Bob, openly expressing her sadness.

"I have an idea," said the ever-accommodating Bob. "Why don't we move to the Netherlands?" he suggested. "That way, we can have the best of both worlds."

"But what about the apartment we have here?" Sue countered. "What would we do with that?"

"We'll keep it, too," Bob answered. "This will always be our home here. We could divide our time between the Netherlands and Canada. I'm not working any more, so what would it matter?"

This sounded like a great idea to Sue, so they began to split their time between the two countries. As Bob said to her, they lived "with one foot in each country." Their official residence was in Edmonton and they bought another apartment in Zaltbommel, about five kilometres west of Rossum, to be near Sue's mother when they were in the Netherlands.

By 1991, Sue had decided she would like to become a Canadian citizen. She had lived in Canada long enough to qualify, so after studying all the information that Immigration Canada gave to her, she made her pledge of allegiance in April 1992. Sue was pleased to receive a brand new Canadian passport to accompany her feeling of pride and gratitude for being able to become a part of the country that had rescued her homeland so long ago.

In Sue's mind, the next logical move was for her to join the Royal Canadian Legion in Olds, Alberta, where Bob and his brother Bill were members. Then she could wear a uniform that matched the one that Bob owned and she could celebrate the annual remembrance days in both Canada and the Netherlands with Bob.

* * * * *

After more than 15 years of travelling back and forth between Canada and the Netherlands, Sue began thinking about a home for her most precious Christmas gift.

"What should we do with the little coat?" she asked Bob one day. "We are coming and going all the time and it's just gathering dust in the closet here in Edmonton."

"What would you like to do with it?" Bob queried back at her.

"I was thinking that maybe we should give it to the Legion in Olds," Sue continued. "Your brother Bill would make sure it was respected."

Bob agreed with Sue's suggestion and approached Bill and the Olds Legion about their idea. On November 12, 2003, the Royal Canadian Legion in Olds, Alberta, arranged a ceremony for the momentous occasion of accepting this special gift.

Sue knew in her heart that she was doing the right thing. People would come to know that this little coat represented the compassion of the Canadian soldiers for Dutch people in their time of dire need. However, handing it over to the president of the Olds Legion was a very emotional moment for her and tears kept welling up in her eyes.

She had kept that "Little Coat" since she was 10 years old – the coat that was lovingly created by the Canadian soldiers at Alphen and given to her on Christmas Day 1944. It was the best Christmas present she had ever received. It was very, very hard for her to part with it.

After its arrival in Olds, the Little Coat told its story every year for the next decade on November 11th, Remembrance Day in Canada. Each year, Bob's brother Bill took the Little Coat to local elementary schools and told the story of its creation to children who were about the same age as Sue was when that beautiful gift was given to her.

* * * * *

On June 21, 2004, Sue's mother Geert Cretier died at the age of 95. She was buried in Rossum alongside her husband Willem in a solemn ceremony.

Both were now gone but never forgotten. Bob and Sue frequently visited their graves.

After moving part-time to Zaltbommel in 1987, Bob and Sue Elliott attended every Liberation Day celebration in the Netherlands. It is a national holiday celebrating the liberation of the Dutch people from Nazi Germany during the Second World War. The tour of army vehicles, soldiers and Canadian war veterans begins in the city of Groningen and travels through a number of other communities throughout the Netherlands.

With each passing year, there are fewer and fewer veterans to march in these parades – a sign that time is taking its toll. In 2005, The Year of The Veterans, the celebrations were extremely emotional for 80-year-old Bob Elliott.

There is a small Canadian flag flying on the grave of Willem and Geert Cretier in Rossum. Bob Elliott placed it there on May 5, 2005, Liberation Day. After placing the flag, he stepped back in his neatly pressed veteran's uniform, came to attention, and solemnly saluted his long-time friends.

Sue watched his display of respect with emotional admiration.

'This is my hero, and he always will be.'

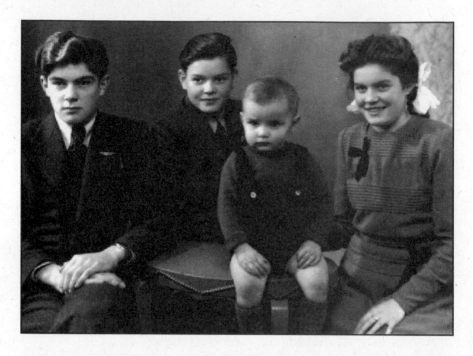

Above: Left to right – Kees, Gerard, Willem Jan and Sussie Cretier, 1948.

Below right: Willem Cretier in a photo shop, Netherlands, 1950s.

Below left: Geert and Sussie Cretier in front of the house that Willem and Geert bought in Hurwenen, Netherlands, after their retirement.

Above left: Geert and Willem Cretier, dressed up for their son Gerard's wedding, Netherlands, 1960s.

Above right: Bob and Sue Elliott on their wedding day, Hamilton, Ontario, Canada, February 1985.

Sue and Bob Elliot, with Sue's little coat in Canada.

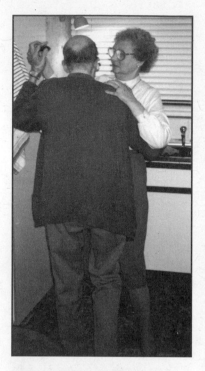

Left: Uncle Archie and Auntie Nan dancing in their kitchen in Scotland, 1998.

Below: Uncle Archie dancing with Sue Elliott.

Sue's granddaughters Mirtaa (age 11) and Iris (age 9) wearing Sussie's little Army-style wool coat.

Above: Bill Elliott shares the story of the little coat with students in Olds, Alberta, Canada, November 2003. Photo by Carla Victor

Left: Bob Elliott at Liberation Day celebration in Waginingen, Netherlands, May 2005.

Below: Bob and Sue Elliott with the Little Coat on display at the Royal Canadian Legion in Olds, Alberta, Canada, October 2005.

Photo – courtesy of Alan Buick

Sue Elliott at her parents' gravesite, Netherlands, May 2009. Note the Canadian flag on the left side of the marker.

Wendy Zuliana of Ontario, daughter of Ernie 'Duke' Dawson, with Bob and Sue Elliott at a Liberation Day ceremony, Netherlands, May 2009.

Epilogue

Alan Buick's interest in the little coat on display at the Olds Legion prompted Bob and Sue Elliott to consider a more prominent setting for this special piece of clothing. In 2006, the Elliotts donated the little wool Army coat to the Canadian War Museum in Ottawa as a permanent reminder of the Second World War and its long-term impact on the people of Canada and Europe.

The coat was carefully restored as one of the museum's dress and insignia artifacts and was placed on display at the Canadian Museum of Civilization in early 2009.

This important piece of fabric had travelled from Canada to the Netherlands in the form of a blanket and then back to Canada as a lovingly-crafted child's coat. It had withstood the test of time and had come to be a symbol of hope during a traumatic period of the world's history.

This little wool coat will remain at the Canadian War Museum and its partner locations to highlight the sacrifices of children and adults around the world in times of combat. It will continue to share yet another inspirational story about the difficult journey towards peace.

Bibliography

The story on these pages is a recollection of the events in the lives of Bob Elliott and Everdina 'Sussie' Cretier (Sue Elliott). Attempts have been made to accurately record and depict these stories. The author has taken some liberties in recreating some of the dialogue for ease of readability.

Details of historic battles and Second World War events were obtained from various Internet resources including:

www.6juin1944.com
www.junobeach.org
www.normandiememoire.com
www.vac-acc.gc.ca
www.historynet.com
www.wikipedia.org

Sue and Bob Elliott with Saskatchewan author Alan J. Buick in Olds, Alberta, Canada, October 2005.
Photo – courtesy of Alan Buick

Author's note

Upon noticing a little coat with Army buttons at the Olds Legion in Alberta in September 2004, I asked my friend Jack Humphries why it was there. The information he gave me piqued my interest and I soon realized there was a story surrounding this tiny article of clothing that had to be told.

My initial investigation revealed that the little Dutch girl who wore the coat in the winter of 1944-1945 and the Canadian soldier who gave it to her were not only still alive and well, but were married to each other! I contacted them and asked if I could write their story. From the moment they agreed to this arrangement, hundreds of e-mails crossed the Atlantic, I met with Bob and Sue at the Olds Legion and finally, with the help of Deana Driver's literary expertise in editing and publishing, we have the book you hold in your hand.

I am thankful for the patience of my wife Carol, as I spent a lot of time over the last five years piecing together this great story. I am also thankful to my stepson Jarrod Hillman for giving freely of his valuable time to digitally enhance many of the old photographs within these pages and for building our web site, www.thelittlecoat.com.

Last but certainly not least, I am deeply grateful to Bob and Sue Elliott for delving into their memories and reliving the terror and sheer horror of their wartime experience so that this true record could be accomplished.

I sincerely wish for all who read this tale of drama, danger, tense excitement and finally, peace, as much adventure as I had in writing it.

May God bless our soldiers for their bravery and compassion.

– Alan J. Buick

From the Elliotts

I see this book as a tribute to all my wartime comrades. It also expresses my feelings for the people of the Netherlands who suffered so much under the Germans during the war years.
I am also thankful I have my Sussie.

Bob Elliott

My gratitude for the young men who gave up their youth and their lives for the freedom of our country. I never, ever will forget.
Veterans, thank you all so very much. You all were heroes and always will be for the Dutch people. I have one veteran for myself and I sure love him.

Much love to you all.

Sussie Elliott